MW00441174

609 LETTER TEMPLATES & CREDIT REPAIR SECRETS

THE BEST WAY TO FIX YOUR CREDIT SCORE
LEGALLY IN AN EASY AND FAST WAY

(INCLUDES 10 CREDIT REPAIR TEMPLATE LETTERS)

BRADLEY CAULFIELD

TABLE OF CONTENTS

INTRODUCTION

Congratulations on purchasing *609 Letter Templates and Other Credit Repair Secrets,* and thank you for doing so.

The following chapters will discuss everything you need to know to finally get rid of some of that debt around you and get your credit score up and doing well in no time. There are a lot of things in our modern world that are going to rely on our credit scores being high and strong, and having a low score from any number of issues is going to be imperative to the success that we can have when taking out a loan, purchasing a home, and so much more. This guidebook will cover all of the tips and tricks that we need to know in order to get started with all of this as well.

The first part of this guidebook is going to spend some time talking about our credit scores and what we are able to do to increase them and make sure they are going to work well for us. If you have a low credit score, this part is going to help you out because it shows the steps we can take to get those scores up to something that will get lenders to look our way.

Some of the topics that we will discuss in this section include what the FICO score is all about, some of the ten secrets of credit repair along with some of the common myths that we need to be careful about to ensure that we can get our score up, what are some of our actions causing harm to our credit score, and even how to pay down our debt to get that score up. We will also take a look at some of the best tips and steps that we can take in order to not only get a good credit score but to get the score up to 800+!

Then it is on to the second section of this guidebook, where we are going to take a look at a little loophole found in the law books. This is completely legal to do, but it is also something that is not well-known, and many people don't realize how they can utilize it for their own needs to clear off their credit reports and get debts to go away. This is known as Section 609, and we are going to spend a good deal of time looking this over and figuring out the right steps to take to make it work for us.

In this section, we are going to take a look at what this Section 609 is all about, what rights it is able to provide to the consumer, and how we can write out some of our own disputes to make sure that we are getting things taken care of and ready to go. We will also look at how to proceed with the letters, what to do if no one responds, and some general advice that will make sure that you can really get the most out of these letters and get someone to respond to you.

You will also find that the third section of this guidebook is going to be particularly useful as well. This is the part where we are going to look at some of the templates of the letters that you can write out. It is sometimes hard to get started with these kinds of letters and to know what to say, and often getting started is going to be the hardest part of all. This section is going to include quite a few template letters that you are able to work with to ensure that you are set and can get started on this in no time.

No one wants to have bad credit follow them forever, and it is not fun to work through your credit and feel like you are not getting anywhere it at all. And in the traditional manner, it could take you months and even years in order to get the score up, especially if you are dealing with some bad collections and judgments that are going on in the past. Working with Section 609 will ensure that things get back on track and can help improve your credit score immensely in a short amount of time.

Many people do not know about the 609 code and may feel that it is a lot of work for just a little bit of profit. But it is a loophole that anyone is able to use, and if it works for you, then it is going to ensure that you are able to get through and clear up your credit score. When you are ready to learn more about your credit score and how it works, and what Section 609 is all about and how it can help raise your credit score, make sure to check out this guidebook to help you get started.

There are plenty of books on this subject on the market, thanks again for choosing this one! Every effort was made to ensure it is full of as much useful information as possible; please enjoy it!

PART 1

ALL ABOUT YOUR CREDIT SCORE

CHAPTER 1

ALL ABOUT THE FICO SCORE

Before we are able to do much about our credit and ensure that it is no longer low and causing us issues, we have to learn more about our credit score. There are actually a few different scores available that we can look through, and each one will rely on a different algorithm to determine how high or low your score is. However, the score that we need to concentrate on is the FICO score. This is the one that most people who will offer you money as a loan will look at, so it makes sense that this is the one that we want to focus on.

WHAT IS A FICO SCORE?

To start with, we need to take a look at what the FICO score is all about. This is a three-digit number that is based on the different information that is found on your credit reports. It is going to help lenders figure out the likelihood that you will repay a loan or not. This, in turn, is going to affect how much you are allowed to borrow, how many months they will give you to repay, and how much you will pay in interest rates or the cost of the loan to you.

Any time that you decide to apply for credit, lenders need to find some manner that is fast and consistent with deciding whether it is a good idea to loan out some money to you in the first place. And it is pretty much guaranteed that they re going to take a look at your FICO score.

A good way for us to think about this FICO score is a summary of your credit report. It is going to take a look at a number of different features, including how long you have had credit, how much credit you have, how much you are using your current available credit, and whether or not you have been good about making payments on time or not.

Not only does this kind of score helps lenders and more make decisions that are faster and smarter about who they will loan money out to, but it is also going to help most consumers get fair and fast access to credit when they need it the most. Because these scores are going to be calculated based on the credit information that pertains to you, you can really influence your own score if you make sure that you don't carry on too much debt, you pay all of your bills on time, and you ensure that all of your choices are smart for your credit.

About 30 years ago, the FICO or the Fair Isaac Corporation debuted these scores in order to provide a good industry-standard for scoring how creditworthy each individual consumer was. This was meant to be a system that was fair to both consumers and lenders. Before this score, though, there were a lot of different scores, and all of them had different methods of calculating how good your score was. In fact, some of these factored in things like political affiliation or gender as well.

The FICO score has found a way to make this a much easier process to work with. Everyone is on equal footing when they start, and then the decisions they make about how much to borrow if they make payments on time, and more, will be what factor into the final score that they get. This makes it fair for both institutions and consumers to rely on along the way.

WHY IS THE FICO SCORE SO IMPORTANT?

There are a lot of benefits to working with the FICO score. These scores have helped many millions of people gain the access they need to get credit for education, to cover their medical expenses, and even purchase their first homes. Even some utility and insurance companies are going to check FICO scores when they decide to set up some of the terms of doing service with them.

The fact of the matter is that having a good FICO score can save you a lot of money in fees and interest along the way because if you have a higher score, it is likely that lenders are going to offer you lower interest rates on the money they lend out. This is because they feel that you present less of a risk to them than others.

An overall, quick, fair, predictive, and consistent score is going to help make sure that the cost of credit to everyone is going to be lower. When the lenders know that their risk is lower, and they do not have to worry as much about people defaulting along the way, then they are more likely to offer lower interest rates to those who are using them and can ensure that we never have to pay more than necessary.

The more accessible credit in general is, the more lenders are going to be willing to loan out, and the more efficient they are going to be in some of the processes that they use in order to drive down costs and pass those savings over to their borrowers.

HOW THE SCORES ARE DIVIDED UP

There are several ways that we are able to take a look at the credit score that comes from FICO. In general, a lender will find that a score above 670 is a good sign of creditworthiness. The higher you are able to get your score, the more luck you are getting loans because you are seen as a lower risk, and it is likely that you will be able to get more loaned out, depending on a few other factors like your income. A good idea of how these credit scores work with FICO includes:

1. Under 580: This means that you have a poor credit score. This is well below the average that most consumers in the US will have, and it shows the lender that you are a risky borrower to give money to.

2. 580 to 669. This means that you have a fair credit score. This score is still below the average for consumers in the US, though it is possible to find some lenders to give out money, especially if you are at the higher end of this range.

3. 670 to 739. This is a good rating for credit score. This is going to fall near and sometimes a bit above the average for the consumer in America. This is the score that most lenders are going to feel comfortable lending money to.

4. 740 to 799: This is the range where your score is seen as really good. Your score is going to be above the average and will show to others that you are a dependable borrower they can trust.

5. 800+: This means that you have an exceptional credit rating. Your score is going to be well above what is considered average, and you can really show off with this score that you are an exceptional borrower who will pay them pack.

THE DIFFERENCE BETWEEN FICO AND OTHER CREDIT SCORES

Another question that you may have along the way is the differences between the FICO score and the other credit scores; some are out there. To get started, these scores are the only ones that are created by the Fair Isaac Corporation, and they are used by about 90 percent of the top lenders when it is time to make lending decisions overall.

The reason for this is that FICO scores are going to be seen as the standard when it comes to making fair and accurate decisions about the creditworthiness of an individual. They have come in handy to help millions of people get the credit they need for many different purposes.

Now there are other credit scores out there, and they can be used in some situations. These other scores are going to calculate out the number they give you in a different manner than the FICO score can. So while it may seem like some of those other scores are similar to what we see with the FICO score, they really aren't. Only FICO scores are going to be used by most of the top lenders you want to borrow from, and while the others can be good for some monitoring of your score, if you would like, the best way to go is with the FICO score.

CHAPTER 2

10 SECRETS OF CREDIT REPAIR AND HOW TO BUST MANY COMMON CREDIT MYTHS

The next thing that we need to look at is how we are able to work on fixing our own credit scores. There are many myths and bad advice out there that keep you from reaching your goals of doing well with your credit and getting it all under control and a higher score in the process. That is why we are first going to take a look at some of the best ways you can work on repairing your credit, and then will explore some of the common credit myths that you likely believe, and that are holding you back today.

SECRETS OF CREDIT REPAIR

1. Work on the credit history

Your credit history is going to take up a significant reason of why your score is stuck at a certain number. Many times, when people are trying to do some work on their credit, they will go through and close down credit lines or take out new debt to help them out. This is a bad thing to do. When you lose accounts or add on a bunch of new ones, it is going to drag down your credit age.

The credit age is determined by the average age of all of your accounts. If you have quite a few on your list that is higher age, but if you then throw in one or two that are just a few months old, it is going to drag you down. Focus on getting that credit history up there a bit more, and don't open up any new accounts and see what a difference it can make.

2. Look to the available credit

One question that a lot of people have when working on their credit is whether opening up a new line of credit or a new credit card would help them out here. However, if you already have some credit going and you feel stretched thin, then this is not the best action plan to take. The reason for this is that you never want to end up using all of the available credit. This is a big mistake that is going to send up a lot of red flags to credit agencies all over. It is better to realize when too much is too much, and just work with what you have for now.

3. Secured credit

Secured credit is something that a lot of people are trying out now. It is a new method meant to help out consumers who want to boost their scores, who do not have any credit to start with, or who are dealing with poor credit. If you would like to seek out a boost in your score, and you think that you can handle the credit, then take a look at a secured credit card.

Basically, these are going to be the same thing as a debit card. However, they will still have the function of a credit card. You will need to make payments on a monthly basis, just like a credit card. And then, the credit agency is going to be able to see that you are working on building or repairing your credit in the process.

4. Dispute

One of the smartest things that you can do to make your credit score go up is to dispute things that are not accurate on the credit report. Sometimes, the report that is out there for you is going to reflect some falsities that are going to harm your credit score. While it may take some time and won't be easy, it is so worth it in order to help you get that score up.

5. The mistakes

If you are in the process of realizing that you need to repair your credit quite a bit, it is also time to realize that you should no longer make mistakes with your credit. Once you have dug that big hole, it is best to stop shoveling and learn how to stay as close to the surface as possible. These means do not try to take out any lines of credit, make payments on time, and always check your report to make sure it is up to date and shows your efforts.

6. Pay down your debt

We will take a closer look at this one as we go through the process a bit more. But the more you can pay down your debt, the better. This is not an easy process, and you will have to give things up and really reign in your spending. The rewards will be so worth it in the end. You can pick out the budgeting or debt payment method that you want to work with, but as you make more of those payments along the way, you get things done on time, and as you are careful about getting the debt paid down, your score is going to go up.

7. Use credit sparingly

Having a large balance on any of your cards (or even on all of them) is going to harm your credit score. It doesn't matter if you pay your bills in full each month or not. That large balance is going to harm the score. The portion of the credit extended to you that you utilize is going to be sent out to the different credit bureaus, and it can make a big difference in your score. The more you can get the debt paid down, the better.

8. Use the buddy system

If you are new to credit, or you are really running into issues getting any credit, and you need help to build things up, you may want to look at the option of becoming an authorized user on the credit card. This is going to ask another cardholder, like your significant other or another family member, if you can get an authorized card on your name but on their account. This is not going to carry as much weight as what we see with having the card for ourselves, but this can help.

Keep in mind that this is going to be a high-risk kind of strategy. You have to come up with a good system and a good reason for the primary cardholder to actually add you to this account. They need to be people who are able to pay their bills on time as well, or it harms you. And you have to pay off everything as well, or you get them in trouble as well.

9. Pay things often

To help you get the best credit score possible, you need to work with as little of the credit available to you as possible. In fact, if you are able to keep your credit utilization below 30 percent, although 10 percent is best, then you will raise your score. If you have a low credit allowance, like $500, then it is going to be even harder to manage this.

One way to make sure that you are able to use the card but not harm your utilization rate at all is to make more than one payment in a billing cycle. You don't have to pay after each transaction if you don't want to, but if you are doing it on a regular basis, you can make sure your utilization stays at the right spot.

10. Strategically open accounts

While you should not go like crazy and open up a bunch of accounts all at once when you want to improve your credit score, you need to come up with a strategic manner to handle these accounts to keep things safe and organized. Applying for any kind of credit is going to be something done sparingly. These applications result in a hard inquiry on your report, and if they are recent, they are going to take a few points off.

If you are working with your credit limits that are low and your spending reduction isn't necessary, you could open up a new account or two to help you to have more credit. But just remember that you should not increase your spending beyond what you are actually able to afford.

COMMON CREDIT MYTHS

There are a lot of myths out there when it comes to how you can improve your own credit and make sure that it is as strong as possible. And watching out for these myths and making sure that you don't fall prey to any of them is going to be critical if we want any chance of increasing our scores and getting the best results in the process. Some of the most common myths out there that we need to work on and look through include:

1. Pre-employment screens use credit scores.

This is a common thing that people worry about. They may have bad credit, but they want to get a job and work on fixing it. Then they are told that they won't be able to get a job because that credit score is too low. However, credit scores are not, and have never been used by employers for these purposes, and employers are not going to have access to these credit scores.

However, credit reports, which are going to be different than the credit scores, can be used for purposes of employment screening, but that only happens if you provide permission for them to access it.

2. Spread out your balances to get a higher score.

Spreading out your balances on credit cards through more than one card can actually end up harming your credit scores. Remember that a lot of the models out there, include FICO and VantageScore, are going to work with a lot of factors in order to determine these scores overall. The second most important out of these metrics is debt load or the amount and type of debt that you are obligated to work with.

The fewer accounts that you have with a balance, the better it is for your credit score. If you have a credit card that doesn't carry a balance, it is going to impact your credit score in a positive manner. This is because those cards are going to have a debt to limit the ratio of 0 percent.

3. The value of your account age is going to be lost when a card is closed.

Closing a credit card account is not going to make you lose out on the value of how long you had that card. Credit scoring models are going to still consider the age of closed accounts when they figure out your credit score for as long as that is still on your credit report. Some of these are going to continue to an age when they have been closed.

It is possible that closing this card is going to impact the score because it takes away the amount of credit that you have. And this is even worse because it messes with some ratios if you still have a balance on those. But it is not going to mess with the age of the account.

4. These scores are only rewarding us for debt.

Credit scores are actually going to reward customers who do not have a lot of debt, and those who have zero credit card debt will be rewarded the most. The belief that you have to carry a lot of debt to have good scores is a false idea, and it is often perpetrated by those who are not going to understand these scores.

5. Once you ruin your credit, you can never rebuild it.

A credit report is more of a history of your credit, and if you give it enough time, credit is something that we can rebuild. It is not just going to show us the way things are right here and now. It is going to keep a long record of all the credit that the individual consumer is going to open up in their name. It is going to show us the items that are inactive and closed as well, but the history is going to stay there no matter what.

Late or payments that are missed can often stay on a report for seven years in many cases. But it is still possible to go through and rebuild credit. You have to take the time to pay all your debts on time, look for some better options for credit, and learn more about how credit and money work. In addition, the longer the credit history can maintain no negative information, the better it is. Even if you do have some negatives on your credit score, the older it is, the less significant it becomes.

6. Checking your report will harm your score.

If a consumer takes the time to access their own report, it is not going to affect their score at all. This is going to be known as a soft pull, and it can show up on a personal credit report, but won't mess with your score. You can take a look at your credit report as often as you would like to make sure that it is accurate and up to date, and there is no missing information on it, and it will not show up on your score.

When you apply for credit, though, the lender is going to pull out the credit report of the applicant, and this will result in a hard inquiry. These are going to be shown to some other lenders who want to look at your report because they can show new debt that doesn't yet show up on the credit report. These are going to affect our credit scores, and if you have too many of these on a report all at once, it can be a bad sign that you are applying for too much credit at once, or that you are being rejected for some reason.

7. Bankruptcy protection is going to be great for those who have large amounts of debt.

We have to remember that bankruptcy is a legal process that is going to relieve a person from paying their debts. Depending on the type of bankruptcy that happens, the person may be in a situation where they cannot pay off any of the debt, and other times, they may repay some of it.

This is not a get free card. It is going to be something that shows up on your report for ten years in some cases and can make it almost impossible to get credit. Consumers should only choose this if they are absolutely out of options, but you will find that working with a credit counselor is going to be a better option to repay the debts and get things under control. In some cases, you can even settle the debts for less than the original amount in order to help save your credit when you get into trouble.

8. It is impossible for you to get ahold of a credit card if you don't already have credit.

Take a look around any university campus, and you will see that this is not true. Students who have just left their homes for the first time and have never had to be responsible for money in the past, and therefore have no credit score, are going to be able to get a credit card.

It is true though that for you to have a FICO credit score at all, you need to make sure that your credit report has a minimum of one account that has been opened for at least six months, and a minimum of one account that has been reported over to the credit bureau's within the past six months. If you don't meet these two requirements, then you are not going to have anything there for the FICO score to be created.

This does make it harder to get a credit card and to start, but not impossible. Everyone has to start somewhere when it comes to their credit scores, so it makes sense that there are a few options available that we can utilize in order to get started. For example, you could get a secured credit card, a card with a low limit to start, become an authorized user on an account that belongs to someone else, or get a cosigner on a credit card with you.

All of these options are going to make it possible for you to get some of the credit you need, even if you are just beginning, and you don't have anything on the report at all. They do require a few more steps and are not as easy to work with as some of the other options that you can see once you have a credit score. But they can definitely help you to get started

9. Not using credit cards is going to harm your score.

Despite this misconception, avoiding your credit card altogether is not going to help with your credit score, either. Sure, if you have a car loan and a mortgage and you have amazing payment histories, you can go through and create a good score here without needing to work with a credit card at all.

However, if you decide to avoid these credit cards completely, there are some ways that this can harm you. First, about ten percent of your score is going to come from your credit mix. This is going to be increased when you have several types of credit accounts ready to go. Also, about 30 percent of your score comes from the amounts that are owed, which will include your credit utilization ratio or the amount of the credit that is available that you are using.

This may not sound like a big deal, but if you do not have any open revolving credit lines, then this category is going to be non-existent. And that is a huge part of your credit score that you are just letting getaway. Without it, it is really hard to raise your credit score.

10. If you are married, you have just one score.

Another common misconception that we need to be careful about is that if you are married, you will only have one credit score that is combined. You are not going to be treated as just one person for credit scoring and some other financial purposes. Depending on your own situation, this could be helpful or a big disadvantage.

For example, if there is one spouse who doesn't have that good of a credit score, but the other spouse has an excellent credit history, the latter spouse is going to be able to apply for loans and credit cards on their own. They would be able to do this without having to factor in the other spouse at all. On the other hand, for purchases that are going to need both spouses' income to get it done, like a mortgage, the credit of both spouses is going to be considered. The only exception to this is if one of the spouses can afford the mortgage just on their income.

11. Credit scores are not going to change all that often.

There are a lot of people who believe that their scores are only going to be updated at set intervals, maybe just once a month or a few times a year. However, it is possible that your credit is updated on a daily basis, as long as there is some new information being added to your own credit report. A quick glance at your FICO score can help you to see that your score can change a bunch of times, even with a slight change in the balance you pay or owe on one of your cards.

12. It is impossible to get a perfect credit score.

As we are going to show in just a few chapters here, it is completely possible to go through and have a perfect credit score. The FICO credit scoring model is going to have scores that will range from 300 to 850. 850 is going to be known as the perfect credit score. And while this kind of score is pretty rare, with only about 1 percent of consumers having it, this doesn't mean that it is unattainable.

In addition, we may be surprised here that there is not really a magic formula that is going to pop up and ensure that you are able to get the perfect credit that you need. You just need to know how the system of FICO scoring is going to work, and then just be smart and use some common sense when it comes to behaving well with your credit.

We need to consider a lot of things when it is time to take care of our own credit and make sure that it is going to behave in the manner that we want. When it is time to increase our scores, we need to recognize what is bad and drag the score down, what is good and will drag the score up, and what are some of the common myths that may be holding us back overall. Having this knowledge is going to make it so much easier to ensure you can get what you want without making your progress go backward in the process.

CHAPTER 3

WHAT IS HARMING MY CREDIT SCORE?

Now that we have taken some time to look at the different things that are going to raise your credit score, we also need to take a closer look at some of the different parts that are going to end up harming the credit scores that we have. If you are in the process of fixing your credit, you want to make sure that you are careful and that you are not going to end up doing something that will harm your credit in the process. Some of the different things that we are able to watch out for when it comes to harming your credit score include:

PAYING LATE OR NOT AT ALL

One of the worst things that you can do when it comes to your credit score is paying late on anything. About 35 percent of your score is going to be about your history of making payments or not on time. Consistently being late on these payments is going to cause a lot of damage to your credit score. Always pay your bills on time, especially your credit card bills.

What is even worse than paying late is not paying at all. If you decide to completely ignore your cards and other bills and not pay them at all, then you are going to be in even more trouble as well. Each month that you miss out on a payment for your credit card, you are going to end up with one month closer to helping your account be charged off.

If you ever want a chance to get your credit score up at all, especially if you are hoping to get it up to 800 or higher, then you have to stop the late payments. This is going to be a bad thing because it shows that you are not willing to pay your money back, and they are less likely to give you some more money in the process.

For those struggling with making payments, whether these payments are often late or they don't come in at all, it is time to get a budget in place. You are living above your means, and this is never a good sign to getting your score up to where you would like. When you are able to get your budget in place and can start paying your debts on time, you will be able to get that credit score higher in no time.

HAVING AN ACCOUNT CHARGED OFF OR SENT TO COLLECTIONS

Next on the list is having your accounts charged off. When creditors are worried that you will never pay your bills for loans or credit cards, they are going to use a process known as charging off your accounts. A charge off means that the insurer has pretty much given up on ever hearing from you again. This does not mean that you are no longer going to hold responsibility for this debt at all. This is actually one of the absolute worst things out there when it comes to your credit score.

Another issue is when one of your accounts is sent off to collections. Creditors are often going to work with debt collectors in order to work on collecting a payment out of you. Collectors could send your account to collections after, but sometimes before, charging it all off. This is never a good thing, even if the account is charged off at that time, either.

If you are to the point of your bills going to collections or being charged off, this means that you have not just missed one or two payments. It means that you have gone so long without paying the whole thing that the company figures they are never going to get it back. Either they have probably written it off as a tax break or they have sold it to a credit collection company that will be bothering you a lot in the future.

This is never a good thing. You are going to be harassed for a long time to come about all of that. And it is going to show other creditors that you have not just missed a few payments when things get tough. It shows them that you fell so far behind that someone else, someone who had given you money in the past, decided to give up on you in the process. This is hard to fight against and is not going to make a new creditor feel like they should loan you the needed money.

FILING BANKRUPTCY

This is a bit extreme that you should try to avoid at all costs. Bankruptcy is an extreme measure, and it is going to cause a lot of devastation to the score that you are working with. It is also going to be on your record for seven to ten years. It is a good idea in order to seek some alternatives, like working with counselors for consumer credit, before filing bankruptcy.

It is best if you are able to do everything that you can to avoid bankruptcy at all costs. It may seem like the best idea to work with. You assume that when you declare bankruptcy, you can just walk away from all of the debt that you have, and not have to worry about it ever again. This is not really how this whole process is going to work for you at all, though.

There are several types of bankruptcies that you can work with, but often you are going to need to go through and pay off as much of the debts as possible. And sometimes, this can be several years of making payments and having your wages garnished and taken away before you can even get to the bankruptcy. You could just pay the debts for that amount of time instead, or make some kind of agreement with the creditors for a lower amount if needed, and now have the black mark of the bankruptcy on your side.

Once the bankruptcy is actually complete, which is something that can take some time, then a new problem is going to occur. You have to then focus on how you will handle the black mark that is on your credit report for quite a bit of time. This could be anywhere from seven to ten years. And you can bet that creditors are not going to look all that kindly at that. You will find that it is almost impossible to get any kind of credit or any other monetary help that you need for a long time afterward.

And if you are not able to get on a budget and actually take control over your debts, you may get it all discharged, but then you are going to turn around, and before you know it, all of your money is gone again, and you are facing bankruptcy again. This is never a good thing. You are not going to be offered the option of bankruptcy multiple times, and using this as a Band-Aid is not going to work.

To avoid bankruptcy, you need to go through and learn how to work with a budget and figure out the best ways to manage your money, no matter what the income is that you are working with. This is easier to manage than you may think and can help you get on a good payment schedule so that you can deal with your debts and get them paid off. The bankruptcy seems like an easy way to get out of the debt, but it haunts you for many years afterward, can make getting credit later on almost impossible, and it will really not solve the underlying problem that got you to this situation.

HIGH BALANCES OR MAXED OUT CARDS

We always need to take a look at the balances that we are going to have on our credit cards all of the time. The second most important part that comes with our credit score is the amount of debt that is on them, and that is going to be measured out by credit utilization. Having high balances for credit cards, relative to the credit limit that you are working with, will increase the utilization of credit and will make your credit score go down. For example, if you have a limit of $10,000 on a card, but the balance is at $9500 or higher, then your score is not going to reflect in a positive manner with this one.

We also need to make sure that we are not maxing out or going over the limit when it comes to our credit cards. Credit cards that are over the limit or that have been maxed out are going to make the credit utilization that you have at 100 percent. This is going to be one of the most damaging things that you are able to do with your credit score. Make sure to pay down those debts as fast as you can to maintain your credit score and keep it from going over the top.

CLOSING CREDIT CARDS

There are a few ways that closing your card is going to end up with a decrease in your credit score. First, we need to take a look at closing up a card that still has a balance on it. When you close that card, the credit limit you get to work with is going to end up at $0, while your balance is still going to be the same. This is going to make it look like you have been able to max out the credit card, which is going to cause your score to drop a bit. If you want to close your account, then you need to make sure that you pay off the balance before you close it.

Another thing to consider is what will happen when you close out your credit cards that are old. About 15 percent of your credit score is going to be the length of your credit history, and longer credit histories are going to be better. Closing up old cards, especially some of the oldest cards, are going to make your history seem like it is a lot shorter than it is. Even if you do not use the card anymore, and there are no annual fees, you should keep the card open because you are really losing nothing and gaining more.

And finally, we need to be careful about closing cards that have available credit. If you have more than one credit card to work with, some that have balanced and some without these, then closing the cards that do not have a balance is going to increase the credit utilization. You can just keep those all out of the way, and see your credit report go up.

NOT HAVING ENOUGH MIX ON THE REPORT

While this is not as big of a deal as some of the other options, you will find that having a good mix of credit is going to be about 10 percent of your credit score at the time. If you have a report that only has one or two things on it, such as either credit cards or loans, then it is likely the score you are working with will be affected in some way or another.

The more you are able to mix up your accounts and get them to have a lot of different things on them, the better. You don't want to overextend yourself, but having a mix of loans, mortgage, credit cards, and more, that you pay off each month without fail, is going to be one of the best ways that you can raise your credit score without causing harm or paying too much in the process.

This does not mean that you should go out and apply for a bunch of different things all at once in order to get your mix up. This is something that often happens; naturally, the longer you work on your credit score. You may have a few credit cards, and then you take out a loan for a car and pay it off. Maybe you need a loan for a vacation or for some home improvement, so you will have those accounts and then get a mortgage too.

As time goes on, these different loans and credit amounts are going to come and go, but they will all show up in the credit mix and can help to increase your score. If you try and increase your mix all at once, you are going to bring up some red flags against your credit, and this can cause some issues as well. Doing this over a few years as you need it is the best way to make sure that your credit score goes up.

APPLYING FOR TOO MUCH

Another thing that is going to count on your report is the credit inquiries. These will take up about 10 percent of the score that you work with. Making several applications for loans and credit in a short amount of time is going to cause a big drop in your credit score along the way. Always keep the applications for credit to a minimum, so this doesn't end up harming you along the way.

In some cases, this is not going to harm you too much. For example, if you have a good credit score and you want to apply for a mortgage, you will want to apply for a few mortgages and shop around a bit. If you do these close together, then it is not going to be seen as bad because the lender will assume this is what you are doing, rather than you taking on too much or that you have been turned down. You can also explain this to them easily if they ask.

For most other cases, though, this is not going to be a good sign. Having all of those inquiries on your score is going to slightly lower it, at least for the short term. And when other lenders see that you are applying for a lot of credit, they will either assume that you are getting rejected and they will wonder why or they will assume that you are taking on too much credit that you will not be able to handle, and they will not want to lend you any money either.

These are just a few of the different things that we are going to work with when the time comes to handle our credit report. Sometimes the things that can harm your score are going to be much more important than the things that are able to help improve the score. Working on both is going to be important when it all comes down to it as well, and knowing how to avoid some of the common things that can ruin your credit in no time is imperative to getting that score up and seeing it work the way that you want.

CHAPTER 4

SIMPLE STEPS TO FIX YOUR CREDIT SCORE

We have spent a good deal of time taking a look at some of the different things that are going to help improve your credit and some of the things that can end up harming your score in the process. We need to make sure that we are careful about making payments on a regular basis, and that we are not letting things stay on our credit if they should not be there. With all of this in mind, we need some quick and actionable steps that we can follow in order to fix up our credit score and ensure that we are set and ready to go with it. Some of the simple steps that we can use in order to get started with improving our credit score include:

Review your reports: All three of the major credit bureau's, Experian, Equifax, and TransUnion, must provide you with a free copy of the report each year, and all that you need to do to get it is ask. You can also work with a few other options, like Credit Karma and more, to check on your report on a more regular basis. Always check this at least once a year. Many times, checking them at different times of the year can help as well because things can change.

If you see anything that is wrong with your report, then dispute it right away whether this is an inaccurate negative mark, late payments, or an account that is not yours. In the past, you had to write letters to the credit bureaus to get this taken care of, but there are now online services that can make this a bit easier. You want to get the most out of this work, though, and kick out the factors that are weighing down your credit score more than others.

For example, start with the derogatory marks like judgments and collection accounts. It is not that uncommon for a collection to show up, especially if there is some misunderstanding between parties along the way. Some disputes are going to take longer to handle than others, but it is always good to go through and dispute anything that is inaccurate in your report because it can only raise the score.

Next on the list is one that works the best if you are sure you can manage your money well. You can ask to increase your credit limits. One factor that is going to rank high on your credit report is your credit card utilization. If you carry a balance that is 50 percent or higher on your cards, then it is going to have a negative impact on your score. One way to improve this, though, is to pay down your balances. If you are working on that and would like to speed it up, you can try to increase your credit limit.

Let's say that you owe about $2500 on a card that has a limit of $5000 on it. If you are able to increase the limit to $7500, the ratio is going to improve right away. The best way in most cases to get this limit increased is to call the card company and ask. If you have a good payment history, many card companies will do this. They want you to carry a high balance because that is the way they are able to make money. Just be careful and don't use the extra limit that is put there because that puts you further in debt and will lower your score some more.

Another way to increase your limit is to open another card. This can help if you have a larger credit card debt that you are trying to pay off. Again, you need to be careful with this one. If you are taking out a credit card or two to help increase your limit and decrease your credit utilization, then take that card and hide it somewhere to never use. If you end up using the new card on top of the old debt, it will not help you out at all.

As with anything, paying down your balances and your debts is one of the best ways to ensure that you are going to be able to get that credit card a bit higher overall. Paying down a percentage of the available credit can make a fast and significant impact on the score that you have for your credit. Try to cut down on your budget as much as possible, sell things, and do what you can to pay down some of those debts.

We also need to focus on paying off the new credit accounts first, especially if they are high in interest. The age of credit is going to matter in your report. Interest rates matter to your bank account as well. If you put $100 each month to pay down the balances (over the required monthly payment), focus on paying those accounts with the highest interest first.

When that is done, then we need to prioritize by the age of the account. You want to pay off all of the newer accounts first so that you can increase the average length of the credit, which is going to help with the score. And you will be able to avoid paying as much in interest with this plan as well.

And of course, the number one best way for you to get through and make sure that your credit score is going to keep on increasing is if you pay all of your bills on time. Even one missed or late payment is enough to harm your score. It is best if you can do everything possible to always get those bills paid on time.

If you do get in a situation where you are not able to pay off all of the bills on time, then you need to be smart about which bills you pay on time and which ones will be late. Your mortgage lender or credit card provider is going to report any payments that are late to the credit bureaus, but cell providers and utilities usually won't.

Section 609 is another option that we can use. This is something that we will talk about in more detail as we go through the other sections of this guidebook. But you will find that it allows us to safely and effectively remove some of the things that are on our credit reports, but should not be there. Taking the precautions.

You have to remember, though, that this process is going to take time. It would be nice if we could turn around and have all of the debt paid off and ready to go. But this is not a reality. We are able to use the Section 609 and hope that it is able to get our debts paid down quickly for us. But if there are some big and legitimate marks on our score, then this is something that we need to handle and be aware of.

The good news is that when we keep up with the work of fixing our credit score, and we don't give up and fall back into our old habits, then we will be able to see some results pretty quickly. You have to follow the steps that are in this chapter, and in this whole section, then you will be able to get that credit score to increase.

When you are able to put all of these parts together, it is much easier to make sure that there is an increase in the credit score that you are working with. You will find that this does take time, and your score is not going to increase overnight. But if you are able to maintain some of these parts and not be late on payments or do other things that are considered "bad" for your score, then you are going to be able to see that score go up in no time.

CHAPTER 5

HOW TO PAY DOWN DEBT

A simple look online will show us that there are so many different ways that you can pay off your debt, and they are all going to work in slightly different manners. As long as they have you paying down your debt and ensuring that you don't take on new debt, without a bunch of risk in the process, then they are good options to work with. You can choose the one that makes the most sense to you.

We are going to spend some time, not looking at a specific plan that you are able to use to pay down your debt. Rather, we are going to focus more on the basic steps that you can take, no matter the kind of debt repayment plan you are using to help make paying your debts off a little bit easier in the long run as well. Some of the steps that we are able to use here include:

STOP WITH THE NEW DEBT

You are never going to get out of debt if you just keep adding to your debt number. It is always best to stop with the new debt and find ways to limit it as much as possible. While most people are not getting the right kind of training in how to handle money, and you may feel like it is impossible to get out of debt unless you are willing and able to go through the retraining process for your financial habits now.

You need to get right into the mix and make a stand against all of the marketers who are interested in trying to take your hard-earned money or offering you some easy financing as well. Keep in mind that while marketers are going to try to convince you otherwise, you really don't need more stuff to make you happy. What you need instead is financial peace of mind.

So, instead of having the temptation around and taking on more debt, cut up your credit cards so you can't use them. Sit down and come up with a budget, and then stick with it. Turn off the social media and the advertisements so that they are not able to control you any longer. This helps to limit the chances when you are tempted to purchase something that you do not need.

RANK THE DEBT USING INTEREST RATES

For this one, we are going to list out all of the debts that we owe, and list out the interest rate that comes with them. The highest interest rate needs to be put at the top of the list. That will be the one that you work on paying off first. Paying off the high-interest debt is going to be the key to what is known as the stack method of debt payoffs and can get that debt gone quickly.

There are other methods that work well too, but these often focus on motivational factors and can be a little bit slower at getting the work done. Interest is going to be a really powerful weapon, and right now, the banks or other companies are using it against you if you don't pay things off. Interest is going to increase the amount that you have to pay back in the end, and often we are not fully aware of how much that ends up being.

Let's say that we have a credit card that has a $10,000 limit on it, and there is 20 percent interest. You decide to just pay the minimum amount of $200 a month. In the end, it is going to take about 9 years and eight months (if you don't put any more money on it). This means that you are going to end up paying the bank $11,680 extra in just interest.

SEE IF YOU CAN LOWER INTEREST RATES

In some cases, it is possible to lower your credit interest rates with the help of a balance transfer. You need to be careful with this one, but it means that you are going to move your debt to another bank, and they are going to offer you a lower interest rate to try and get your business.

If you are going to do this, you don't want to just jump right in. Make sure that you are going to actually pay the amount off rather than end up with two credit cards that are maxed out. And you should shop around to get the lowest amount of interest for the longest duration possible. Read through all of the terms and conditions that show up as well to make sure the bank doesn't have hidden fees or other issues that you need to be worried about.

CREATE YOUR OWN BUDGET

This is where we are going to work on improving our own financial control. We need to bring out some pen and paper and write down what your total income is, after-tax, and then write down all of the expenses that we have. This includes any of the extras that you have and the minimum payments that you owe on as well. We can cut these out later, but we just want a full look at it to start.

We can then look at all of the expenses that are there and rank them based on how important they are. Look at the items that are near the bottom of that list and determine if they are worth cutting to keep you financially stable. The objective here is to create a plan where you can get the expenses lower than the income.

You also need to go through and figure out how much you are willing to spend on all of the areas of your life. You can set aside amounts for eating out, groceries, rent, buying clothes, and more. Once you allocate that money, though, realize that you are not allowed to dip into other areas, and you are done at that time. You may want to consider working with a fun account that will be there just for you to spend on something that doesn't usually fit into the budget. This allows you a bit of freedom without derailing the budget.

Even if your expenses are already below your income when you start, this doesn't mean that you can just stop here and call it good. You want to make sure that you can cut your budget down as much as possible. This allows you to make more money each month and throw it at your debt payments, making it more efficient and getting that credit score in line faster than ever.

CREATE YOUR OWN REPAYMENT SCHEDULE

The first part that we need to focus on here is covering at least the minimum on all of the debts you have. If you miss anything, even if you are trying to pay off another debt faster, you are going to incur a lot of feed and more, and these can add up quickly. Make at least this payment each month.

Then, you take the debt that has the highest interest rate, and you will use the extra that is found in your budget and pay that extra towards that biggest debt. As you see, the official minimum payment goes down, and you will be able to add the extra to your target debt. This will help you to really pay down the debt pretty fast, especially if you put any extra money towards that each month.

When that first debt is all done, then it is time to move on to the second-highest interest rate debt. With this one, you will take the minimum payment that you were doing before, along with the minimum payment that is available from the debt you paid off, and any extra you were paying. All of that goes towards the second debt, and that can be paid off in no time.

We continue this process, taking the extras that are used from one debt and throwing them at the next one on the line, with the payments getting bigger and paying things off faster as we go along. While the first debt may take some time to complete because you are also paying on all of the other debts, but by the time you get to the last few, they will be paid off in no time.

BE KIND TO YOURSELF

Keep in mind that paying off debt, even though it is so good for your credit score, is not something that you are going to be able to do overnight. During this process, which can be a long one, you will feel that your resolve is going to be tested quite a bit. You may have an emergency that happens, like a car breaking down, and you will have to change your plans a bit.

This is a normal part of life and not something to get really frustrated about. The important thing to remember here is to not give up and revert to your old habits, or you will never get that debt paid off. Be kind to yourself when things in life happen, but don't give up. You will get those debts paid off in no time if you are willing to do the work.

The reason that we want to work so hard at paying down our debts and making sure that they don't stick around for a long period of time is that it helps us with our credit scores while freeing up more money to do what we want. When our utilization rates are lower because we pay things off, and we don't miss payments because the amounts are not as high as they were, then our credit score will go through the roof.

CHAPTER 6

CAN I REALLY GET MY CREDIT SCORE TO 800+

Now it is time for the hard part. Maybe you have been doing some of the work that we go through in this guidebook, and you have seen a nice increase in the amount of your FICO score. This is always good news, but now we want to take it further and see if we can get our score to 800 or higher. Only the elite have this kind of score. It is hard to get because it requires a perfect balance of types of credit, a high credit limit, and no missed payments, among other things. But it is possible.

When you are able to get your credit to be this high, it is a lot easier for you to go through and actually get credit and loans at any time that you would like. If a big calamity hits you and you have a bunch of medical bills to deal with, then this credit score can help you to take care of that and somewhere that will benefit you as well like if you would like to start a business, get a new house, or do something else along the same lines, then this high of a credit score can help you.

So, how do we make sure that we are able to get our credit score up to 800 or higher? The first thing is to know the facts. Once you are able to answer the main question of "What is a perfect credit score?" you will find that it is easier to take on the right steps in order to figure out exactly what you can do to reach the perfect score. First, though, we need to make sure we know where we stand on the FICO scale.

Once a year, you can get a free annual credit report from any of the country's top credit bureaus, all three of them. If you go through this and find any issues on any of them (sometimes a mistake will show up on one and not on the others), then this is the time to fix them. You will never get to an 800+ score if there are a bunch of errors in your report.

The next thing that we can focus on is establishing a long history of credit. Most of the time, with a few exceptions, lenders are going to view borrowers with short histories of credit as riskier to work with. To reach a credit score that is 800 or higher, you have to establish, and then also maintain a long history. So even if you are not using some of the accounts, keeping them open will help you to get that score up.

As we have mentioned a bit before, you need to make sure that all of your bills are paid on time. There isn't a single person who has an 800+ credit score who also has a missed payment, or a bunch of missed payments, on their report. Paying your bills late or not paying the bills at all is going to decrease your score. If you have trouble remembering the due dates, then consider signing up so that you can have automatic payments and have that taken care of for you.

We also need to take the time to redefine our credit card usage. About 30 percent of the score you have will consist of the utilization rate for your credit, which is going to be the amount of debt you owe divided by the total credit available. Typically, we want to stay under 30 percent, but if you are trying to get a higher score, then staying under 10 percent is best.

One thing that we have not talked about much in this guidebook yet, but will help you to get that higher score you want, is to learn how to diversify the accounts that you are holding onto. This is one of the best ways to strengthen your credit, and while this can take some time to accomplish this, you will find it is a great way for us to make sure that our credit score is able to go up.

You can make your credit score stronger when you are able to diversify your accounts. This is not an excuse to go out there and open up 10 different card accounts at a time. What it means is that you should have a mix of different types of credit, such as an auto loan, a student loan, a mortgage, and a credit card. Ten credit cards are not going to be a diverse mix of debt and responsibility with your score. But having a bunch of different accounts, even if some of them have been paid off, is going to be a much better option to work with.

While you work on your credit score, you need to make sure that you can cut your spending and create a budget that you are able to stick with. This helps you to stay within means that you can afford and makes it less likely that you are going to fall into trouble with your spending. Although it is true that your credit is not going to factor in your income, living within your means, no matter what that number is, is a great way to raise your score.

Next on the list is to find ways that you can limit the liability that you are dealing with. When you go to co-sign a loan, remember that this may seem like a nice thing to do, but you are really taking on a risk for another person. If you do this for someone who is not able to manage their debt all that well, it is going to negatively affect your score because you will be responsible for that debt as well. If you want to make sure that you can get a credit score that is 800+, and maintain that, then it is a good idea to avoid co-signing at all.

In addition to this one, you should make sure that your liability is limited in other manners as well. You should always report your cards that have been lost or stolen right away. If you don't do this, then it is likely that you will be liable for any of the purchases that are not authorized at the time. And if you are not able to afford those purchases, then your score is going to be the thing that suffers here.

And finally, we need to make sure that we are restricting the hard inquiries that happen to our report. Whether it is you or another agency or institution who is pulling out the credit report and asking for a copy of it, you are dealing with an inquiry. A soft inquiry can happen on occasion as well, and it is generally not going to be enough to make any changes to your credit. This soft inquiry is going to happen when one of the following occurs:

1. You go through and do a check on your own credit report.

2. You give an employer you may work with in the future permission to go through and check your credit.

3. You have the financial institutions that you do business with go through and check your credit.

4. You get a credit card offer that has been preapproved, and that specific company goes through and checks your credit.

While the soft inquiry is not going to do all that much to our credit scores, we do need to be careful about the hard inquiry. This is going to be the one that is able to affect your credit score. This is when a company is going to pull up your credit report after you apply for a product like a credit card or a mortgage. You want to make sure that you can limit the hard inquiries as much as possible to get the best results with this.

PART 2

THE SECTION 609 CREDIT REPAIR SOLUTION

CHAPTER 7

WHAT IS SECTION 609?

In the previous chapters, we took some time to lookup more about what we can do about our credit scores, how to keep those scores as high as possible, and many more. The good news is that building up your score is not something that has to take years, and it doesn't even need to take months as long as you are prepared and able to make this work well. In fact, there is going to be a loophole that we are able to take advantage of in Section 609 in the Fair Credit Reporting Act that is going to help us to get a higher score as quickly as possible.

Yes, this is going to sound like it is too good to be true. But you can rest easy knowing that it is something that you can use. It is open to anyone, and if you are paying for the services to get it done, then that person is scamming you, not this part of the code.

The point of this loophole, or at least the way that you are able to get it to work for you, is that it is going to place the burden on the credit bureaus and targets some of their own internal practices and policies. Before we get into the different details that we need to know about this section 609 and how we are able to use it for our needs, we first need to take a closer look at this section and how we are able to use it here.

WHAT IS SECTION 609?

The first thing that we need to take a look at here when it comes to our credit scores is what Section 609 is really all about. This is going to be one of the best ways for you to get your credit score up, and outside of a little calling or sending out mail, you will not have to do as much to get it all done. Let's dive in now and see if we are able to learn a bit more about it.

The FCRA or the Fair Credit Reporting Act, is going to cover a lot of the aspects and the components of credit checking to make sure that it is able to maintain a reasonable amount of privacy and accuracy along the way. This agency is going to list out all of the responsibilities that credit reporting companies, and any credit bureaus, will have. It also includes the rights of the consumer, which will be your rights in this situation. This Act is going to be the part that will govern how everything is going to work to ensure that all parties are treated in a fair manner.

For example, when we are using this Act, the consumer has to be told if any of the information that is on your file has been in the past, or is now being used against you in any way, shape, or form. You have a right to know whether the information is harming you, and what that information is.

In addition, the consumer is going to have the right to go through and dispute any information that may be seen as inaccurate or incomplete at the time. If they see that there are items in the documents they are sent, if the billing to them is not right or there is something else off in the process, the consumer has the right to dispute this and the credit reporting agency needs to at least look into it and determine if the consumer is right.

Other issues that are addressed in this Act are going to be done in a manner that is the most favorable to the consumer. This Act is going to limit the access that third-parties can have to your file. You personally have to go through and provide your consent before someone is able to go through and look at your credit score, whether it is a potential employer or another institution providing you with funding.

They are not able to get in and just look at it. Keep in mind that if you do not agree for them to take a look at the information, it is going to likely result in you not getting the funding that you want, because there are very few ways that the institution can fairly assess the risk that you pose to them in terms of creditworthiness.

Along with some of the other parts that we have discussed above, the consumer does have the option to go out and seek damages from those who violate the FCRA if they can prove that it happened. There are a number of ways that a credit agency can go through and break or violate the FCRA, so this allows the consumer a way to protect themselves if that proves to be something that needs to happen.

Another thing to note about all of this is that the FCRA is going to be divided into sections. And each of these sections is going to come with a unique set of rules that all credit bureaus need to follow. In particular, section 609 of the FCRA is going to deal with disclosure and is going to put all of the burdens of providing the right kind of documentation on the credit bureaus.

This may sound a little bit confusing, but it means that you may have debt or another negative item that is on your credit report, but there is a way to get around this without having to wait for years to get that to drop off your report or having to pay back a debt that you are not able to afford.

Keep in mind that this is not meant to be a method for you to take on a lot of debts that you can't afford and then just dump them. But on occasion, there could be a few that you are able to fight and get an instant boost to your credit score in the process.

You do not have to come up with a way of proving whether or not the item on the credit report is legitimate or not. Instead, that is up to the credit bureaus. And there are many cases where they are not able to do this. Whether they brought the debt and did not have the proper documentation, or there is something else that is wrong with it, the credit company may not be able to prove that you are the owner of it or that you owe on it at all. If this is the case, they have to remove the information from your credit report. When a bad debt is taken off, or even a collection is taken off, that does nothing but a lot of good for your overall score.

We are going to take some more time in this section to look over the Section 609 from the FCRA. But this is the basics of what you need to know. It is going to be a useful tool, as long as you work with it well and learn how to make it work for your advantage, and can raise your credit score by quite a bit.

WHY USE A 609 LETTER?

The 609 Letter is going to be one of the newest credit repair secrets that will help you to remove a lot of information on your credit report, all of the false information, and sometimes even the accurate information, thanks to a little loophole that is found in our credit reporting laws.

If you have spent a bit of time trying to see some increase in your credit score, you may find that the 609 letter is the right thing to do to get some of the negative accounts, the ones that are pulling your credit score down quite a bit, taken from your report. You can use this kind of letter in order to resolve some of the inaccuracies that show up, to dispute your errors, and to handle some of the other items that could inaccurately come in and impact and lower your credit score.

When it is time to report your credit history at all, one of the credit bureau's is going to be responsible not only to include information that is verifiable but also accurate in the report. The use of this letter in credit repair is going to be based mostly on the idea of whether the credit bureau was responsible for how they verified the information they put onto the report and if they can do it in a timely manner.

Credit bureaus are going to collect information on consumer credit from a lot of different sources like banks, and then they are going to be able to resell that information to any business who would like to evaluate the consumer credit applications. Credit bureaus are going to be governed by the FCRA or the Fair Credit Reporting Act, which is going to help detail what credit reporting agencies and information furnishers can, and can't, do when they decide to report information on the consumer.

Using this 609 letter is a good way for us to clean up our credit a bit, and in some cases, it is going to make a perfect situation. However, we have to remember that outside of some of the obvious benefits that we are going to discuss, there are a few things that we need to be aware of ahead of time.

There are few limitations that are going to come with this as well. For example, even after you work with the 609 letters, it is possible that information that is later seen as accurate could be added to the report again, even after the removal. This is going to happen if the creditor, after the fact, is able to verify the accuracy. They may take it off for a bit if the 30 days have passed, and they are not able to verify at that point. But if the information is accurate, remember that it could end up back on the report.

New debt collection agencies could go through and add some more outstanding debts to your credit report at any time. This could bring the score back down, especially if you are not careful about how you spend your money and handle debts along the way.

While some people think that it is possible, keep in mind that you are not able to eliminate any obligations to repay a debt that is legitimate. Even if you write out a 609 letter and you are able to get that debt removed from the credit report, whether that is for the short term or a longer-term, you still have to pay that legitimate debt. Don't use this as a way to hide from your debts or get away from paying them at all. Use this as a method that will help you to clear out some of the older options, or some of the debts that you have taken care of, but still remain on your reports.

In addition, contrary to some of the myths that are out there when it comes to these 609 letters, the FCRA is not going to require that any of the credit agencies keep or provide signed contracts or proof of debts. However, you can ask them to provide you with some kind of description of the procedure that they used to complete the investigation into your accounts.

The FCRA, though, is going to give you as a consumer the right to go through and dispute some of the errors that show up on your credit report. This is not a way for you to go through and make some of your student loans or other debts go away, so you don't have to pay them any longer. But it is going to be one of the best ways that you are able to get information that is not accurately taken off the credit report.

We are able to get a lot of things done when we work with the Section 609 letters, but they are not a magic pill that will make things disappear for us. They will make it easier for us to go through and get rid of information that is not correct and can ensure that we are able to get rid of debts that maybe we settled in the past, but are still harming our credit. This is going to make it easier overall for us to really ensure that we are able to get things organized and get a higher credit score that we are looking for.

CHAPTER 8

WHAT ARE MY RIGHTS UNDER 609?

We spent a bit of time in the previous section looking at Section 609 and what it means for us. We are going to dive into it a little bit more at this point and explore how it can be the thing that we need in order to help us get our credit scores up and doing well, without having to wait months or even years to make it happen.

To start, the FCRA is going to be something that works focusing on the rights of the consumer. Rather than being on the side of the credit agencies, this is a whole thing that focuses on the consumer, making sure that their rights are being respected, that the credit agencies have to keep up with good practices, and more.

The FCRA is going to focus on the consumer and their rights, from having the right to know all of the things that are in your own file to have the right to ask for your own credit score when you want to see how it is doing. In particular, Section 609 is going to center on the right of the consumer to verify the accuracy of accounts that are showing up, or debts that are attributed to them.

This means that all agencies have to be able to verify and disclose all relevant information when it is asked. This can be done when there is a case of identity theft for the individual. But we can also go through and use this when there is a dispute of inaccurate or incorrect information on the report.

There are a number of rights that the consumer gets to enjoy when it is time to work with Section 609 for their needs. To start with, some of the excerpts that we are able to see with Section 609 will include:

"A consumer reporting agency shall provide to a consumer, with each written disclosure by the agency to consumers under this section." Some of the things that the consumer reporting agency then has to provide will include:

1. A statement that a consumer reporting agency is not required to remove accurate derogatory information from the file of a consumer unless the information is outdated under section 605 or cannot be verified.

If there is old information on your account, especially if it is derogatory, then you can change it. If you have paid off the debt and you and the debtor have agreed that it is done and should be erased, then the credit agency has to remove it as well.

Keep in mind that there has to be a reason for the removal. Section 609 is not going to erase something from your account just because it is derogatory, and you don't want to have it there any longer. If there is a loan on your account that is delinquent and you still have not paid it off, then that information is going to stay there. And if you are not able to prove in some manner (and this could be the credit agency calling the debtor to confirm, but not being able to get ahold of them), then you are going to have to keep it on as well.

On the other hand, if there is a derogatory mark that is not accurate at all, or it is considered to be outdated for some reason, then the reporting agency has to go through and remove it. If they are not going to remove it, especially after a request, then they will send out a statement to let you know what account, details about the account, and the reasons for not removing that account from your credit report.

2. As proof of positive identification of the victim, at the election of the business entity.

This is sometimes going to be used as a way to prove your identity with an employer. There are not as many who choose to work with this because it can be seen as discrimination in some cases and causes many hassles. But if you have looked for a new job and the employer has gone through and used this as a way to identify you, then the credit agency has to let you know about it.

Of course, if you applied for a new job and gave permission to that job to go through and look at your credit score, this notification is not going to be that big of a deal. But if someone else is using your information to take out credit or get jobs, or a business decides to violate the rules and pulls out your credit report without your approval, this letter would be one of the first hints that something is going on in this manner.

3. As proof of claim of identity theft, at the election of the business entity.

We are also able to work with our credit report and see everything on the report, for free, any time that there is suspicion of identity theft. When you think that this is an issue for you, then getting ahold of your credit report and seeing what is on it can be super important. It will ensure that you can find the information that is accurate and take off the information that was not yours. And often, this is going to be the first sign that something is wrong with your credit, so seeing this report is necessary.

The credit agencies traditionally offer one free credit report a year. But if you are a victim of identity theft, they have to provide you with another copy, even if it has been less than a year since the last time you requested yours. And if there is proof that there has been some identity theft, then the credit agencies need to work with you in order to get things back in order and take off the accounts that are not yours.

In addition to the parts above, Section 609 is going to state "The Bureau, in consultation with the Federal banking agencies and the National Credit Union Administration, shall prepare a model summary of the rights of consumers under this title with respect to the procedures for remedying the effects of fraud or identity theft involving credit an electronic fund transfer, or an account or transaction at or with a financial institution or other creditor."

This is the part that is meant to protect you if there is something going on with your credit that is not your fault.

Checking your credit report on a regular basis, though, and making sure that no one is getting your information and wrecking your credit is the best way to protect yourself. Going ten years without ever looking is a surefire way to get someone to take over your identity, and can make it harder to prove later on that you had no idea what is going on.

Being proactive and watching your credit report as much as possible is not obsessive. It is a way to ensure that you are able to take care of yourself and get those bad accounts off before they ruin your credit and make it even harder to fix things.

While all of this information is going to relate in a direct manner to the rights that you as a consumer are to expect from other credit agencies, that is not the main focus that we need to be on here. Instead, we are going to shift our focus to what all of these have to do with the responsibilities of the reporting companies and credit bureaus and why this is beneficial for you.

With this in mind, we need to take a quick look at why this Section 609 is a good thing for those who are trying to raise their credit scores, or even for those who are just trying to make sure that bad things on their report will not harm them too much.

The other part of this chapter is going to seem like a ton of legal jargon, and like it doesn't make a lot of sense. But when we look a bit closer at how this works, it is a great way for you to get out of bad credit. To help us understand how this is going to work, we need to break down the ideas of Section 609 piece by piece and see what we are able to do with it.

The first thing to consider is that the lender never actually sends the application of credit to all three of the credit bureaus, even though the law that we are talking about before requires that this verification is done before we are able to add it to our report. This is a simple fact that a lot of people are going to overlook. But most lenders are just going to send out to one, maybe two, of the main agencies.

Because the lenders are not going through and actually verifying with the three agencies, it is a technicality that we are able to use in order to get some of the negative points that are on our reports taken away from the credit score. In addition, it is also going to be the bureau's obligation to make sure that consumers know all of their rights, and this is something that often gets put off as well.

In addition to some of the points that we made above, as one of the excerpts of Section 609, you need to have your identity verified before any of the information is included on your report for credit. If you have a debt that is negative but has been on your report for a long time, it may be easier to argue that the collections companies or the credit agencies are not able to prove whether or not that debt is yours.

There are some instances where the bureaus are going to fight on this one. But if the debt is older, then they may figure it is not worth it, and that too much time has passed, so they will just write it off and take it off your account. At the very least, it is worth your time to give it a try and see whether or not it is going to work. It could be the trick that you need actually to get your debts taken off and increase your score.

As a result of this process, the debt can often be taken away from your report, and all you had to do is bring it up to the right agencies. Remember that it is your right, thanks to the rules of the FCRA, to have any unverifiable or inaccurate information removed or corrected in other necessary manners, from your credit report.

Basically, the reason this is going to work for your needs is that there are a few smaller technicalities through this Section 609, including the ones that we listed out above, that you are able to argue in order to take some of the negative items out of your report and delete them from your score. In some cases, it is possible to have student loans, and some other debt, taken away from your credit report altogether, saving you time and hassle and even money.

This is all done legally to help get the work done. And it is a good loophole that you and others are able to work in order to get your debts taken care of and to ensure that you can improve your credit scores. It doesn't always work if you go after the wrong kinds of debts, and you don't understand how the law works; you could end up with some issues. But when this is used in the right manner, it is going to provide us with a good way to make our credit scores better.

The other sections that we will spend some time working with are how we can write out a dispute on this kind of law, and the best ways to include the right things in our dispute letters. We will also look at some of the tips and other guidance that we are able to use in order to work effectively on the dispute and ensure that we are able to get this all set up and ready to go.

Working with Section 609 is not meant to be difficult. And if we are able to learn how to use it in the proper manner, it can get rid of some of the bad debts and other parts that are found on our credit reports. Luckily, it is all completely legal to work with. We just need to understand how the law works, how we are able to utilize it for our own needs, and even what needs to be found in the templates we are working with. We will even take a look at some of the templates that we are able to use to get this done and make sure that we can delete some of the different negative parts of our credit score.

CHAPTER 9

HOW CAN I WORK WITH 609 TO FILE A DISPUTE?

At this point, it is likely that you are really excited to get started. You have heard a little bit about Section 609 and how great it is. Maybe you have been working really hard on clearing out your debt and trying to get it under control in a manner that is efficient and will help you to see good results in the process. Or maybe you just are tired of having a bad score, and you want to see what Section 609 is able to do to help you get things under control.

That is why we are going to spend some time in this chapter, taking a look at how we are able to work with Section 609 and make it work for cleaning up our credit reports. We have already taken a look at how much we are able to do with this part of the law, and some of the benefits to consumers. So, let's take it a little bit further and look at some of the specific ways that we can use this section of the law to help us file a dispute.

Now that we know a bit more about Section 609 and what it is all about, how do we go through the steps and actually do something about it? What is going to be the best strategy to work with to make sure that we reach someone and that our request is taken care of? There are a lot of people who have used this, and sometimes they get results that are a bit mixed. But with the tips in this chapter, you will be able to increase your chances of making this work well.

First, we need to look at the difference between sending a letter into the credit agency and filing complaints. While filing a complaint is often a lot faster and easier to work with, letters are going to be the best route to go with here. And there are a few people who have tried to file a complaint with the FTC or Federal Trade Commission when it comes to their credit reports, but this is not the best route to go.

For those who decided to go with this route, they all received a generic statement that basically told them how the FTC is not going to intervene in any dispute between the credit bureau and the consumer. What this basically means is that if you try to file a complaint, you are going to be all on your own.

A much better method to use and one that is going to ensure that you are actually going to reach someone who can help and won't ignore you is to write dispute letters that will reference right back to Section 609. We will provide a few templates that you can use later on to do this, but if you are uncertain about the steps to get this done, it is also possible to hire a lawyer who is able to help you fight against the credit bureaus.

If you can do this in the right manner, you will find that sending out a well-written and well-organized letter will help you get some good results. You need to state your opinion and mention the right parts, but it is something that you are able to accomplish.

The best way to work through this is to pick out some sample letters and templates to get it all done. This will ensure that you don't miss out on any of the parts that are necessary to talk to the credit agencies and can help you know where to start. In a few chapters, we are going to take a look at some of the best templates that we are able to utilize in order to send in this dispute letter so that you can send in the one that has to do with your complaint the most, or the one that fits your style the best. Use these to make sure that you format and then draft your own personal letters.

However, before we jump to that part, we need to have a few things organized and ready to go. We need to make sure that we have, in our possession, so we can look at them, a copy of each of the credit reports from the three main agencies. This is because we want to be able to go through and dispute all of the negative items on those reports within reason.

Being able to look back at the reports on a regular basis to check on information and make sure they are accurate is going to be important to get them taken care of in your dispute. As you will see pretty soon, the key to writing out a dispute letter that is effective and able to get the job done is going to be in having to present enough details.

The number one thing that we need to include when we are working with this dispute letter is that you need to reference, in specific, the FCRA, and the Section 609 in it before it is effective. Along with proving your own identity, you will find that mentioning both of these parts will be a big part of the dispute you are trying to work with.

If you are still a bit uncertain about where you should start, or if you are getting started on this dispute letter and find your mind goes blank when you want to write, the sub-sections below are going to provide you with a good outline or a good list of all the things that we want to include in our letter. Some of the points that we want to keep in mind as we go through all of this will include:

1. Again: reference back to Section 609. In all of this, you want to make sure that you directly cite and then quote Section 609 in the letter that you send out to the credit bureau. This is going to be a good way to reinforce that it is your right here to come in and dispute the different items that are on the report. This is going to be the best way to show the other side that you actually know what you are talking about.

2. Request receipt of delivery; When it is time to mail out this letter, you need to make sure that you ask for a delivery of receipt. This is just an added protection that will ensure the company will not be able to claim later on that they didn't receive it.

3. Save everything: This is going to require a lot of organization on your part. You need to make sure that you keep some detailed records of the whole process of a dispute. Make a copy of any letters you send out for your own reference, note the dates that are important,

and keep all of the files that are related to one another. You can even keep some of the electronic copies in a folder that is specified on your computer and back it up to keep things safe.

4. Include some kind of proof of your identity: You always want to make sure that you include some proof of your own identity with each and every correspondence that you send. Section 610 (a) (1) of this FCRA is going to stipulate that consumers have to provide the proper identification in order to get a response from a credit bureau. If you do not send these along (we will include some good examples in the next chapter), then the bureau is not even going to take a look at the letter at all, and they definitely will not take a look at your case.

Now, we also need to take into consideration the timeline of your letter. Section 609 of the FCRA is going to contain another key element that is going to make it easier to win any kind of dispute that you want to do. All disputes must be addressed within 30 days, or all of the disputed information that you sent and talked about in the letter has to be deleted from the files.

Now, this can be extended in some cases, such as up to 45 days, if more information is found in the process that will lead to a re-investigation. This can be something that is worth your time to try, though, even if your case may not seem all that strong to start with. If the agency does not respond or is not able to prove whether you are right or wrong within the 30 days, then the information has to be deleted from your report.

Say that you are going through this process, and you are a bit unsure about whether your case is solid and strong enough to go against the credit agency, even if you brought up a not so strong argument, if you do not get a response from that agency within 30 days or less, then that information has to be taken from the report.

This may not seem all that important, but it can help to make sure that time is on your side, and it is something that you may want to include in the dispute letter that you are sending out. The main thing that comes up here is the idea of technicalities, and you definitely want to make sure that they work out in your favor and not in favor of the credit agencies.

Think of it this way; does anyone really care that not every single piece of every single credit file has been verified by numerous sources? For the most part, no, no one really cares about this. However, you do have a right, thanks to Section 609, to dispute it, and this is something that is often going to work in your favor when it is all done.

For the credit agencies, there are a lot of times when they will just let it slide, as long as it is something that is not that big of a deal. This is because they are dealing with the reports of millions of people, and they just do not have the time or the resources to take a look at all of them. If your dispute is small enough and isn't something like getting rid of bankruptcy, then it is likely that the 30 days will pass, and you can say goodbye to that one thing, or even a few things in some cases, that is holding your credit score back.

Following Section 609, Credit Repair method has been able to make a big difference for a lot of people when it is time to raise their credit scores. People report that their negative items or the accounts that are disputed on the report have been deleted, and this has caused their credit scores to improve by quite a bit. It takes a bit of time and the right template and format in order to accomplish this, but it is basically a simple letter and waiting for a bit of time, and you could live free from the burden of bad credit and enjoy the benefit of good credit in the process.

In the next section, we are going to take a look at some more of the specifics of what we should add into our reports, and into the disputes, to make them stand out, and to ensure that no one is going to be able to take the rights of Section 609 away from us.

CHAPTER 10

WHAT DO I NEED TO INCLUDE IN MY DISPUTE

The next thing that we are going to take a look at here is what we need to include in our 609 Letter. The more details we are able to include in this letter, the better it will be for us overall. We don't want to prolong the process because the credit bureau is not sure what we are talking about, and we don't want to raise up any red flags at all. When we send out some of these letters, we want to make sure that the dispute has the right information in place to help us see results.

When we are writing out some of the dispute letters, it is important that we go through and include all of the information that is relevant to our needs, along with a few other key elements, so that we can get a letter that is impactful and effective all rolled into one. A strong letter is not only going to help make one of the best cases for you; it is going to make sure that you are able to hit on some of the points that you would like to emphasize and will tie all of this information back to the specific parts of Section 609 that you would like to highlight at this time.

A strong letter is important because it will ensure that you are noticed along the way. A weak letter is going to get you, at best, a form letter. And this is definitely not what we want when we work with our dispute letters, so we need to make sure that we get it right the first time.

With this in mind, we need to make sure that we include all of the background information that is necessary and the supporting information in order to reinforce and support the dispute that we are doing. The checklist that we are going to work on below is going to help us remember a few of the things that we have to remember when we want to write out our letter including some of the basic information, the documentation that we need, the right wording to get it done, how to reference the FCRA and so much more.

First, we are able to start with some of the basic information. This is pretty simple to work with, but it will include your full name, the account information if you have it readily available, and your own personal information for them to contact you. If you are working through this with a legal representative, then you should make sure to include their contact information as well.

Then it is time to bring in some of the relevant documentation. For each of the credit bureau's you would like to contact, you need to make sure that you are providing some kind of proof of your own identity along with the letter. The good news is that there are a few different options you can choose to help prove this one, including any documents that are able to verify your full name, your date of birth, and your social security number. Some of the options include:

1. A copy of your driver's license

2. A social security card

3. Passport

4. Marriage certificate

5. Birth certificate

6. One of your W2 forms if it has your social security number on it.

You need to make sure that the verification that you want to use here is going to have your full name and your SSN on it. You also need to have some documents that are going to verify what your most current mailing address is. This could be found on the house deed, the mortgage, utility bills, rental agreement, driver's license, and more.

And of course, we need to make sure that we go through and have a copy of our credit score. You are not going to get very far if you do not have this credit report ready to go. You also need to go through and have all of the relevant items highlighted on it to keep it ready and organized.

We have to make sure that we are working with the right references, statements, and wording to make this work. A mention of Section 609 that we are dealing with here and the exact portion that you would like to reference in your letter will be important. Each portion that you want to mention is going to be denoted with some combination of an uppercase, and a lowercase letter, a number, or some kind of Roman numeral based on what it is all about.

For example, if you would like to go through and reference part of 609, and the part we want to work with would start with "Summary of rights required to be included with agency disclosures," you would want to call it paragraph (c) (2) under Section 609 to help them see what you are talking about in all of this.

Another thing to include here is a call to action. This is going to be the specific language that you are able to use to help describe what you would like to see happen next. If you would like to get clarification on something, then state that in this part. If you would like to see something taken off the report, then you need to talk about that. It is important that, at some point in the process, you state what you are specifically looking for when you talk to the credit company.

There can also be a statement that is going to explain to the credit company that all of the issues that you outlined in your dispute need to be addressed within 30 days or less. This is going to be a critical part of taking advantage of the loophole that is found in Section 609 for the timeline of these disputes in the first place. Sometimes this can be the saving grace that you are looking for when it is time to get that thing run off your credit report.

As you are writing, you should work with as many words as you can to reinforce some of the gravity of the situation that is going on. This will help to show that you are serious about working with this and that you are actually knowledgeable about this situation, rather than just trying to fool them and get rid of something that should legitimately be there.

For the most part, you are going to submit the dispute by mail. When it is time to go through and submit your dispute letter, it is best to send it by mail and do it by certified mail if you can. You can even request that there is a return receipt for you to have on your records. This is going to be a good way to make sure that the credit company can't come back and say that they didn't receive the letter. You should also make sure that anything you send out goes to the right department, so it reaches the right people. This should be the complaint department.

From here, it is up to the credit company to figure out how they are going to handle the dispute. Each company is going to do this in a slightly different manner based on what is best for you. It is also possible to work with these disputes online if you would like, but the preferred method is often going to be with sending through the mail.

The thing to remember here is that one of the keys to doing an effective letter of the dispute is to be specific, have attention to details, and include accuracy. Using a polite but firm tone is going to be really important with this as well. If you work with a letter that is angry, including a lot of exclamations and name-calling, this will not be taken seriously and could get you into a lot of trouble at the same time.

Along the way, make sure that you get it all proofread and fact-checked along the way. When you are done with the original draft of your dispute, you should have someone you trust to look through it. This allows for some proofreading and fact-checking as you go through, and will make sure that you have gone through and included everything. Pay attention to the grammar and spelling that you use because this will be important to get a concise and clear message across. If you send out a letter that has a lot of mistakes, you will not get the results that you want.

And then remember to be persistent. It is possible that you are going to need to send out more than one letter to get the results that you want. With each of these letters that you send out, you need to make sure that you include all of the documentation that is required again, especially when it comes to the proofs of your address and your identity. If you do not receive a response, then there is going to be a template in our final section that will make it easier to draft the follow-up letter that you need.

Finally, we need to remember that even if we do this work and we are not able to get our score to increase, that doesn't mean that everything is all lost here. There are still other actions that we are able to take to improve your credit and help improve your life in the process.

CHAPTER 11

GENERAL ADVICE TO SEE SUCCESS WITH 609

Whether you want to delete just one thing from your record or you are looking to delete a lot of different things at the same time, you want to make sure that your 609 Letter is taken care of and ready to go. There are a lot of parts that need to go through in order to get this done, but when you look at some of the templates that we have in the next section, you will see that this is not as bad as it may seem.

When you are ready to write out some of the letters you need to send out to the credit agencies, and you are getting all of the documentation ready to go, make sure to follow some of the general advice that we have below:

KEEP ALL OF THE RECORDS

Everything has to be recorded on your end of things. Don't just send out a letter and then assume that it is going to be all good. You never know when things are going to go missing or when you will need to prove your side of things. And the more accurate and in-depth records you are able to keep, the better it will be with everyone.

This means that we need to keep track of everything, from the moment that we start sending out information and letters to the credit bureaus all the way until way after they take that information off your credit report. This will help you if anything comes back later on, or you need to make sure that you can prove your side of the story if the credit agency doesn't respond or do what they are supposed to.

Keep track of everything that you can along the way. You should have all of the letters that you send out, both the originals and any follow-ups that you send as well. If the credit agency gets in touch with you, then you should keep the letters they send to you and your responses back. You can hold onto all of the supporting documents that you send each time as well. The more information that you add to your records about this, the better it will be for getting your way in the process.

ADD IN THE IDENTIFICATION INFORMATION

Before you send out any information or work with section 609, make sure that you send along with it some identification information. This is going to make sure that the credit agency is going to understand who you are and can prove that they are actually working with the person who says they own the account or at least own the SSN that goes with all that information on the credit report.

There are a lot of different options that you are able to use for showing your identity, and you should include a number of them with your letter to help prove who you are. You would want to work with information like your driver's license, social security numbers, and more to showcase who you are and why you need to make a difference in the credit report.

CONSIDER BRINGING SOMETHING UP, EVEN IF IT DOESN'T SEEM IMPORTANT

While you are at this process, it is worth bringing up even some of the smaller things that are on your report. Even if these don't seem important at the time, and they are not the main thing you want to put your time and attention on, while you are writing the letter, you should add in as many details and as many disputes that are legitimate as possible.

You never know what you would be able to get erased off the credit report, and how much of a difference that is going to make to your credit score along the way. Even if the item seems small, you should consider adding it to the dispute.

Sometimes, the time limit will go on too long, and the agency will not respond. If this happens, all of the items, whether they are big or small, will need to be taken out of the report. And you will find that even a few small things can add up to be big things in the long run. Even if the credit agency won't erase all of the little things, it doesn't really take much of a difference along the way in terms of the time that you take to get it all done. And it could make a difference.

DO NOT CONTACT THE FTC

One thing that a lot of people are going to try and use is to contact the FTC and other agencies in the hope of getting things fixed. They may hope that because there is something wrong with the credit report, the FTC will be able to help them take care of this. Sometimes they are mad and want to get the agency in trouble for falsely adding things to their reports. And other times, they may just not know who they are supposed to contact.

However, this is not going to do you any good. If you contact the FTC, they are not going to be able to provide you with the assistance that you need. In fact, their stance is that they are not going to get in between you and the credit agency at all, and all you will get back is a form letter stating these facts. Since you have other options at your disposal to work with, you do not need to work with the FTC, but just make sure that you are going not to waste time in the process.

When you want to get something on your credit report fixed and all better, then it is important not to waste time with the FTC, and instead go straight to the credit agencies. You can send the same letter and the same information to each one, and they are the ones who will be able to help us to get things done. If you follow the rules that we are using here, and some of the other steps that we talked about in this section, you will be able to get your credit report taken care of.

SEND A LETTER TO EACH CREDIT AGENCY

One thing that we need to remember here is that we have to go through the process of sending out one of these Section 609 letters to each credit agency that we want to get to remove the items. The credit agencies are not going to talk to one another about this. If you send out a letter to Transunion, but not to one of the others, then Transunion may take it off your report, but none of the others would do this for you.

You have to be responsible for sending a letter to all three of the reporting agencies if you would like to get that debt taken out of all of your reports. You should automatically send this information to all three right from the start, so make sure to get copies of all the information so that you are ready to go and handle all of that at once as well.

You can include the same information in each of the letters that you send out. And you can even send out the same letter, just make sure to change the company and department name that you are using on each one. Then include the same proofs of your identity, the credit reports, and more, for each one to get the ball rolling here.

MENTION SECTION 609 IN THE LETTER

There are a few different things that we need to remember when it comes to writing out our form letters. We need to include our name and some of the information about who we are and where we live. We need to include information about the debts and accounts that we would like to dispute along the way, including a credit report to show what accounts were talking about. And then we need to make sure that we, at some point, mention the section 609 in the letter.

This is going to be useful in several aspects. First, it is going to show the credit agency that you know what you are talking about. There are a lot of people out there who would like to fix their credit scores, but they don't understand the laws, or they are trying to sneak past things. The credit agencies are going to notice these individuals easily and will not want to work with them at all.

But when you go through and mention the Section 609 in your letter, like we have talked about so far in this guidebook, then you will find that it is much easier for you to grab their attention. You actually have done your research, you know what your rights are, and you are ready to take them on to get the credit report taken care of. The credit agencies are going to notice and respect this, and that will make it more likely that they will listen to you and send out the information that you need or erase the information that should not be there.

MENTION THE 30-DAY LIMIT

In addition to making sure that you mention something about Section 609 in the letter you send out, you also need to make sure that you mention the 30 days that the agency gets to respond to you. This not only helps to show that you have a good idea about what you are talking of here but will make it easier for you to remind the credit agency about this right that you have with the Section 609 that we talk about here.

The letters that we have below are examples of how you can write these out in your own form letter. But make sure to mention that you expect the credit agency to respond and work with that time limit in order to get things taken care of. If you do this, then it is a lot harder for them to come back with not knowing about the time limit, and sets out the same expectations that everyone on both sides needs to follow.

USE ONE OF THE TEMPLATES, SO YOU KNOW WHERE TO START

Making sure that you have all of the right parts show up in your letter is going to be a challenge. You want to make sure that you write it out in the right manner, that you mention the right parts about Section 609, and you want to make sure that you sound like you know what you are talking about along the way.

The good news is that we have provided some templates that we are able to use in order to take care of this process. There are several Section 609 templates that you are able to work with at the end of this guidebook, and they will be able to provide you with the right way to word your letters to get them noticed. They will mention the Section 609, the FCRA, and even the 30-day notice that is important so that you can really write out a letter that is going to get noticed and can help you to clean out your credit report.

SEND A FOLLOW-UP LETTER

We may think that all of the work is done, and we won't have to do anything else after we send off the initial letter to all three credit agencies. But unfortunately, there are a few other steps that we need to complete. Once you are certain that the 30 days have passed and you have given the company enough time to respond to what you sent in, it is time to send in the follow-up letter telling them that it is now their responsibility to remove that information from your credit report.

We are going to provide you with a good template that you can use at the end of this guidebook for the follow-up letter. But it will basically tell the agency that you sent in information about the different disputes you had on your credit report, and since they have not replied in the timely manner given by the FRCA in Section 609, it is now time for them to remove those items from your credit report.

These letters are short and sweet and will not have a lot to them. They will summarize some of the information that you sent out to them a month ago, and then reiterate what your rights are under Section 609 and what you expect the credit agency to do now that the right amount of time has passed. Depending on the length of your original dispute, this letter could be long or short.

There are a lot of misconceptions out there when it comes to working with the Section 609 letter, and getting it right is going to make the difference between whether you are able to get the credit agency to do what you would like, which would then increase your credit score, or not. Following the advice in this chapter will help you to make this whole process easier as well.

CHAPTER 12

HOW TO PROCEED WITH THE LETTERS

Now that we know a little bit more about the Section 609 and how we are able to use this for some of our own needs when it is time to handle our credit report and get the different parts to increase, it is time to look at how we can proceed with these letters.

In the following section, we are going to take a look at the steps that you can utilize in order to write out one of these Section 609 letters. But then it is time to figure out what we want to do with them when the letter is written. There are a few different ways that we are able to make sure these letters get back to the right parties, and we are going to take a look at all of them below:

EMAILS

Our world seems to run online all the time, and finding ways to work on our credit scores and not have to waste a lot of time copying things or worrying about the paper trails can seem like a great idea. And in some cases, we may find that sending in our 609 letters through email is going to be the best situation for our needs.

Before you do this, though, make sure that you take the time and do the proper research. You want the forms to end up in the right locations, rather than getting sent to the wrong departments, and not doing anything for you in the process. Most of the time there will be listings for the various departments that you want to handle and work with for each credit agency, so take a look at those.

Again, when you are ready, you need to have as many details ready to go for this as possible. Just sending in a few lines about the process and thinking that will get things done is foolish. Write out a letter just like you would if you planned to send these by mail, and use that as the main body of your email. Mention Section 609 and some of the disputes that you want to bring up.

In addition to this, you need to take some time adding in the other details. Attach some ways to prove your identity to the email, along with a copy of the credit report that has been highlighted to show what is going on and what you would like to dispute. Add in any of the other documentation that is needed to help support your case, and have it as clean and organized as possible to make sure the right people can find it and will utilize this information to help you out.

DOING IT ALL ONLINE

Many of the credit agencies have made it easier to go through and work on some of these claims online. This helps you out because you will not need to go through and print it all off or worry about finding the paperwork or printing a bunch of things off. And if you are already on your credit report, your identification has been taken care of.

Since so many people are online these days, doing this right from the credit report is a simple and easy process to work with, and you will catch onto it fairly quickly. Don't take the easy way out with this. If you just click on the part that you think is wrong and submit a claim on it, this is not enough. There won't be any reference back to Section 609, and you will not be able to get them to necessarily follow the rules that come with Section 609.

This is where being detailed is going to be useful in the long run. When you do submit one of these claims online, make sure that you write a note with it to talk about Section 609, specifically the part of 609 that you want to reference in this dispute. You can usually attach other forms to document, who you are and why you think these need to be dropped.

Treat this just like you would if you tried to mail the information to the credit agency. The more details that you are able to include in this, the better. This will help to build up your case and can make it harder for those items to stay on your credit report for a long period of time. Make sure to mention the 30-day time limit as well.

TELEPHONE

A telephone is one method that you can use, but it is not usually the right one for this kind of process. For example, how easy is it going to be to show the credit agency what your driver's license looks like? You can repeat the number over if you would like, but this process is still a bit more laborious than some of the others and doesn't always work as well as we would hope it could.

However, this is definitely an option that we can use in order to reach the credit agencies, and for some people who are not sure of what their rights are, or would rather talk directly to the individuals in charge about this issue, the telephone can be the right option. Make sure that you have a copy of your credit report in front of you when you start and having some other identification information and more. This will ensure that you are prepared when someone comes on the line to speak with you.

Just like we will show when working on our letter templates, later on, we need to make sure that we speak about the issue at hand, explain our rights, and go through the information on Section 609. There is the possibility that the other side is going to have some questions for you, and they will at least want to go through and verify your identity to make sure they are ready to go. But the same rules apply here, and if you don't get a response within 30 days of that phone call, then the information should be erased.

Keep good records of what is discussed in that conversation, who you talked to during that time, what time and date it was, and so on. This will make it easier to get someone to respond to you and can help us to get this to work in our favor. Also, remember that you will need to repeat these phone calls to all three credit bureaus in order to get your information cleared on all of them.

MAIL

Another option that you are able to work with is mail. This is usually a good method to use because it allows you a way to send in all of the information at once. Since you probably already have a physical copy of your SSN, driver's license, the credit report and more, you can get copies of these made pretty quickly, and then send them on with the Section 609 letter that you are working with. This method also allows us a way to go through and circle or highlight the parts of our credit report that we want to point out to the credit reporting agency.

This method is quick and efficient and will make sure that the information gets to the right party. You can try some of the other options, but sometimes this brings up issues like your information getting lost in the spam folder or getting sent to the wrong part. Mail can take some of that out of the way and will ensure that everything gets to the right location at the right time.

CERTIFIED MAIL

For the most part, you are going to find that working with certified mail is going to be one of the best options that you can choose. This will ensure that the letter gets to the right place and can tell you for certain when the 30-day countdown is going to begin.

If you send this with regular mail, you have to make some guesses on when the letter will arrive at the end address that you want. And sometimes you will be wrong. If there is a delay in the mailing and it gets there too late, then you may start your 30 days too early. On the other hand, if you assume it is going to take so many days and it takes less, you may wait around too long and miss your chance to take this loophole and use it to your advantage.

Certified mail is able to fix this issue. When the credit agency receives the letter, you will get a receipt about that exact date and even the time. This is going to make it so much easier for you to have exact times, and you can add these to your records. There is no more guessing along the way, and you can be sure that this particular loophole is going to work to your advantage.

Another benefit that comes with certified mail is that you make sure that it gets to its location. If you never get a receipt back or get something back that says the letter was rejected or not left at the right place, then you will know about this ahead of time. On the other hand, if it does get to its location, you will know this and have proof of it for later use.

Sometimes things get lost. But you want to be on the winning side of that one. If the credit agency says that they did not receive the letter, you will have proof that you sent it and that someone within the business received it and signed for it. Whether the company lost it along the way, or they are trying to be nefarious and not fix the issue for you, the certified mail will help you to get it all to work for you.

When it comes to worrying about those 30 days and how it will affect you, having it all in writing and receipts to show what you have done and when it is going to be important, this can take out some of the guesswork in the process and will ensure that you are actually going to get things to work for you if the 30 days have come and gone, and no one will be able to come back and say that you didn't follow the right procedures.

As we can see, there are a few different options that we are able to use when it comes to sending out our Section 609 letters.

PART 3

THE TEMPLATES YOU NEED

Before we get started here, there are a few tips and rules that we need to follow in order to make sure that we are going to get the most out of the templates that we want to use. We are going to take a look at a number of different letters and templates that we are able to send out to the agencies that report our credit so that we can dispute some of the debt or the negative items on our reports. All of these are going to be easy to tailor and will talk about Section 609 to make it a bit easier for you.

There are a few tips that you are able to follow to make these work for your needs as well. First, make sure that when you get started on this that you are as thorough as possible. Any time that you want to go through and draft one of these dispute letters, you need to make sure that you include in as much information as you can. And, whether you do these correspondences through email or mail, keep all of the records in case you need them later on.

If you are in doubt about something, then you need to include some documentation. You need to include all of the information that is relevant to help move this process along and prove your own identity. Having information on your driver's license for proof of your identity, a copy of any documents that you received, and more details about the dispute that you are working with. So, if you have an account that has been listed as being late in the past, then you would want to go through and print out all of the statements and the records that are recent that show the payments that you have been able to work with.

And we need to take the time to illustrate our case as much as possible. This means that the more details that we are able to show, the better. Include details, including explanations, all of the dates that you can, and your account numbers. This is going to show that you really did some homework before you got started and that you are taking this whole process as seriously as possible.

As we mentioned a bit before, the disputed information will need to be taken from your report within 30 days if the credit agency doesn't go through the process of responding to you. It can be extended to 45 days in some cases if there ends up being the need for a re-investigation to look into it a bit more.

With this in mind, we also need to take a look at what is found in each template. Each of the templates will be on their own, but the fourth one is going to be a good template to use as a follow-up after trying one of the first three templates that we are working with. The others are going to include some variations that we are able to focus on based on the words that you would like to use and the tactic that you want to handle.

Use these templates in the rest of this section to help you compose and keep your dispute as organized as possible. When you pay attention to some of the details that are there, you are going to find that it is easier to come up with a letter that is direct, convincing, and effective.

TEMPLATE #1

This is the first template that we are going to spend some time on. It is going to include all of the different parts that you need in order to get the message to the right parties, and it is nice and simple. Remember that this is just a template, and we are able to go through and use this as a guide or an outline. If it does not exactly match up with what you want, you can make some changes, or you can choose to use one of the other templates that we will have available.

Name

Address

Phone Number

Account # (make sure to include this if you have that information).

Name of the Company Contacting/Point of Contact Person

Relevant Department

Address

Date

Dear [Include the name of the credit reporting agency or use the name of the contact party if you have access to this information]

I am writing today to exercise my right to question the validity of the debt your agency claims I owe, pursuant to the FCRA, Fair Credit Reporting Act.

As stated in Section 609 of the FCRA, (2) €:

"A consumer reporting agency is not required to remove accurate derogatory information from a consumer's file unless the information is outdated under Section 609 or cannot be verified."

As is my right, I am requesting verification of the following items:

[This is where we are going to list any and all of the items that we are looking to dispute, including all of the account names and numbers that have been listed with your credit report]

Additionally, I have highlighted these items on the attached copy of the credit report I received.

I request that all future correspondence be done through the mail or email. As stated in the FCRA, you are required to respond to my dispute within 30 days of receipt of this letter. If you fail to offer a response, all disputed information must be deleted.

Thank you for your prompt attention to this matter.

Sincerely,

[Add your signature to this part]

[Print your name here]

See attached; [This is where you are going to list out all of the documents that you are going to attach with this letter]

*Make sure that you attach copies of your proof of identity, including your birth date, name, SSN, and your current mailing address. You also want to attach a copy of your credit report, making sure that you highlighted all of the relevant items to make it easier for the interested parties to see what you are talking about.

TEMPLATE #2

There are a lot of times when the first template that we discussed is going to be enough for your needs and can help you to get all of the work done. On the other hand, it may be possible that you want to talk about the dispute in a different manner, or you just did not like the setup or something else about the other template that we went through. That is just fine. The following template is going to be the one that we can work with as well. It talks about a lot of the same issues that we did above but will have a few other parts added to it to make this work as well. The second template that we are able to work with includes:

Name

Address

Phone Number

Account # (make sure to include this if you have that information).

Name of the Company Contacting/Point of Contact Person

Relevant Department

Address

Date

Dear Sir or Madam

I am writing to exercise my right to dispute the following items on my file. I have made a note of these items on the attached copy of the report I have received from your agency. You will also find attached copies of documents that help to show my identity, SSN, birthdate, and current address.

As stated in the FCRA, or Fair Credit Reporting Act, Section 609:

[This is going to be the section where we include a few relevant quotes that are based on what area of Section 609 you would like to dispute at the time. You can go back to the previous chapter to see what some of these quotes are all about, or you can go to the FTC's website to get the official document that has the exact verbiage that you need. Remember that you need to note which of the sub-sections you are quoting from as well].

The items that I wish to dispute are as follows:

1. [This is the part where you are going to include as many relevant items as you can. You can have up to 20, but try to only work with the ones that make the most sense for you].

2. [Keep in mind that the details are going to be the most important with this one. You want to include the name and the number of the account, as listed on your credit report]

These are [inaccurate, incorrect, unverified] due to the lack of validation by numerous parties that is required by Section 609. I have attached copies of relevant documentation.

I would appreciate your assistance in investigating this manner within the next 30 days. As required by the FCRA, if you fail to do so, all aforementioned information/disputed items must be deleted from the report.

Sincerely:

[Add your signature to this part]

[Print your name here]

See attached; [This is where you are going to list out all of the documents that you are going to attach with this letter]

*Make sure that you attach copies of your proof of identity, including your birth date, name, SSN, and your current mailing address. You also want to attach a copy of your credit report, making sure that you highlighted all of the relevant items to make it easier for the interested parties to see what you are talking about.

TEMPLATE #3

We have taken a look at some really good examples of the template that you are able to utilize when it comes to working with Section 609 and making sure that you can get the credit agencies to erase some of the bad stuff that is on your reports and causing you a lot of issues along the way. However, we are going to take a look at a third template that we are able to use as well.

You will see that this one is going to be pretty similar to what we have done in the last two, but there are some different ways to present the information and different words that are being used as well. Let's take a look at this example and see how it can be similar or different from the other two templates that we are working with:

Name

Address

Phone Number

Account # (make sure to include this if you have that information).

Name of the Company Contacting/Point of Contact Person

Relevant Department

Address

Date

To whom it may concern,

This letter is a formal dispute in accordance with the Fair Credit Reporting Act (FCRA).

Upon review of my credit report, I have found that there are several inaccurate and unverified items. These have negatively impacted my current ability to receive credit, and have provided unnecessary embarrassment and inconvenience.

As I am sure you are aware, it is my right, according to Section 609 of the FCRA, to request a proper investigation into these inaccuracies. In particular, I am referencing Section 609 (c) (B) (iii), which lists "the right of a consumer to dispute information in the file of the consumer" under the "model summary of the rights of consumers."

As such, the following are items I wish to dispute on my credit report:

1. [This is the part where you are going to include as many relevant items as you have. You can do up to 20. Make sure that you include the name and the number that is listed on each account on this report.]

I have also highlighted all of the items that are relevant to the attached copy of the said credit report.

As stated in the FCRA, you are required to respond to my dispute within 30 days of receipt of this letter. If you fail to offer a response, all disputed information must be deleted. I have attached all the relevant documentation for your review. I thank you in advance for your prompt response and resolution of this issue.

Sincerely

[Add your signature to this part]

[Print your name here]

See attached; [This is where you are going to list out all of the documents that you are going to attach with this letter]

*Make sure that you attach copies of your proof of identity, including your birth date, name, SSN, and your current mailing address. You also want to attach a copy of your credit report, making sure that you highlighted all of the relevant items to make it easier for the interested parties to see what you are talking about.

TEMPLATE #4

This is going to be a slightly different kind of letter than what we saw before. This is going to be important because it helps us to follow up if we have not heard anything from the other party. Remember that we are giving them 30 days to go through and provide us with a response of some kind, or they automatically have to take that off their reports. The 30 days begins when they get the letter you send, not when you write it or when you send it. This is another reason why it is important to go through and get it sent through certified mail, so you have an exact date in hand.

When the 30 days are done with, it is time to do a follow-up letter. This is going to be when you let the agency know that the 30 days are over and that you expect things on your report to be erased and done with as soon as possible. That is why we are going to work with the following to help us write the follow-up letter that we need.

Name

Address

Phone Number

Account # (make sure to include this if you have that information).

Name of the Company Contacting/Point of Contact Person

Relevant Department

Address

Date

Dear Sir or Madam

My name is [Your name], and I reached out to you several weeks ago regarding my credit report. This letter is to notify you that you have not responded to my initial letter, dated [insert date]. I have restated the terms of my dispute below for your convenience.

[This is where we are going to insert information from the letter we wrote originally about the disputed items. Include disputed account names and numbers as listed on your credit report.]

Section 609 of the FCRA states that you must investigate my dispute within 30 calendar days from my initial letter. As you have failed to do so, I kindly request that you remove the aforementioned items from my credit report.

Any further comments or questions can be directed to my legal representative, [insert name], and I can be reached at [insert phone number].

Sincerely

[Add your signature to this part]

[Print your name here]

See attached; [This is where you are going to list out all of the documents that you are going to attach with this letter]

*Make sure that you attach copies of your proof of identity, including your birth date, name, SSN, and your current mailing address. You also want to attach a copy of your credit report, making sure that you highlighted all of the relevant items to make it easier for the interested parties to see what you are talking about

TEMPLATE #5

We also want to make sure that you can have as many of these templates available that work for you. You could try sending a different one to each of the three credit agencies if that works the best for you, or you can choose to send the same one to all three. No matter what options you are considering here, we need to make sure that we are able to get a lot of choices in the process. Here is the fifth template letter that you can consider using for your needs.

Date

Your Name

Your Address

Your current city, state, and zip code.

Complain Department

Name of Credit Bureau (You can pick which one goes here)

Address

City, State, Zip Code

Dear Sir or Madam

I am writing to dispute the following information in my file. The items I dispute are also circled in the attached copy of the report I received. (Take this time to identify all of the items that you would like to dispute, going by the name of the source including whether they come from a tax court or creditors and so on. You can even identify the type of item that you refer to, such as a judgment, a credit account, and more.)

This item is (incomplete or inaccurate), because (take this time to describe what is wrong with that item and why.) I am requesting that the item be deleted (or you can insert the other course of action that you would like to see), as per Section 609 of the FCRA.

Enclosed are copies of (use this sentence if applicable and describe any of the information and documentation that you enclose, such as court documents and payment records), documentation to support my position.

Please take the time to investigate this matter and delete the disputed items. As per Section 609 mentioned above, you have 30 days from the receipt of this letter to respond, or the item must be removed. I appreciate your speed in this matter.

Sincerely

[Add your signature to this part]

[Print your name here]

See attached; [This is where you are going to list out all of the documents that you are going to attach with this letter]

*Make sure that you attach copies of your proof of identity, including your birth date, name, SSN, and your current mailing address. You also want to attach a copy of your credit report, making sure that you highlighted all of the relevant items to make it easier for the interested parties to see what you are talking about.

Template #6

This one is going to be a little bit different compared to the other letters that we worked on, but it is still going to mention the right parts of the Section 609 that are needed to ensure that we are able to take care of everything and to make it more likely that the credit agency is going to do what we request in the process. The good news is that there are a few different things that we are able to do with this one, and in particular, this one is going to be there to help us handle fraudulent charges.

If you actually have a fraudulent charge on your account, and you are not just trying to get the numbers in your favor and get the credit agency to delete something that may be a little bit inaccurate or not in your best interests, then you will definitely need the Section 609 and this template to help. This is what Section 609 was originally made for in the first place, even though some parts of it allow others to get help as well. If you are working with some fraudulent behavior on your accounts and you would like to get it taken care of right away, then check out this form letter.

Date

Your Name

Your Address

Your current city, state, and zip code.

Complain Department

Name of Credit Bureau (You can pick which one goes here)

Address

City, State, Zip Code

Dear Sir or Madam

As I already reported through telephone (if you are dealing with identity theft, it is likely that you spent at least a little bit of time talking to several credit agencies on the phone), I am a victim of identity theft. I have recently learned that my personal information was used to open an account at your company.

I did not open this account, and I am requesting that this account be closed and that I will be absolved of all charges on the account. This is made pursuant to Section 609)e) of the Fair Credit Reporting Act.

Pursuant to federal law, I am requesting that you provide me and/or the listed Law Enforcement Designee, at no charge, copies of application and business records in your control relating to the fraudulent account and/or transactions. A copy of the relevant federal law is enclosed.

My Law Enforcement Designee is:

(include their name, address phone number, and email along with any other information that is important here.)

Pursuant to the law, I am providing you with the following documentation, so that you can verify my identity:

1. A copy of my driver's license (you can also include another identification card that has been issued by the government.)

2. A copy of the police report that pertains to the identity theft.

Please provide all information relating to the fraudulent transaction, including:

1. Application records or screen prints of Internet/phone applications

2. Statements

In addition, due to the regulations set out by Section 609, if this problem is not addressed within 30 days, the disputed item (s) must be removed from my credit report.

Sincerely

[Add your signature to this part]

[Print your name here]

See attached; [This is where you are going to list out all of the documents that you are going to attach with this letter]

*Make sure that you attach copies of your proof of identity, including your birth date, name, SSN, and your current mailing address. You also want to attach a copy of your credit report, making sure that you highlighted all of the relevant items to make it easier for the interested parties to see what you are talking about.

GOODWILL LETTER

Date

Your Name

Your Address

Your current city, state, and zip code.

Creditor Name

Creditor Address

RE: Regarding a Reported Delinquency

To Whom It May Concern

I am (insert name), and my account number is (insert your account number here). I have been a satisfied customer of (add in the name of the creditor) for (X number of years).

Your outstanding customer service is the reason that I have stayed a loyal customer. I have always found it a priority to make all my payments on time. However, in the past few months, I have fallen short of my own standards, and I was over a month late (or another length of time late) with a payment.

I had been carrying a sizable balance for several months. Then, I finally paid off the full balance in February. When I got statements from your company in March, and then in April, I threw them out because I assumed they would have a balance of zero with no payment due to me. I did not think that there could be a finance charge left from that final month that had a larger balance.

I realize that looking back, I should have anticipated that charge. I wish I had taken a moment to open and read those statements, and that was a mistake on my part. I will always open every piece of mail that I receive in the mail from you. I recently opted into email alerts to help provide an added layer of protection for this.

Your records will show that I had never been late with payment until this unfortunate oversight. I have been prompt with the past two monthly payments since getting caught you.

As a long-time customer in good standing, I respectfully request that you apply a goodwill adjustment to remove the late payment of this file.

Thank you for your consideration,

Sincerely

(Your signature)

(Your printed name)

CEASE AND DESIST LETTER

Date

Your Name

Your Address

Collection Agency

Collection Agency Address

RE: Account # (add in the number of your account)

Dear Sir or Madam

Under the Fair Debt Collection Practices Act Section 805 (C), it is my right to request that you cease your contact with me. I am using this letter to exercise my rights. I formally request here that you immediately CEASE and DESIST all contact with me.

With this notice, under the current law, you can only contact me from here on:

TO advice me that your company's further efforts are being terminated;

To notify me that your company may invoke specified remedies which are ordinarily invoked by such debt collector or creditor, or

When applicable, to notify me that your company intends to invoke a specified remedy. GIVE THIS LETTER THE IMMEDIATE ATTENTION IT DESERVES

Sincerely

(add in your signature)

SECOND GOODWILL LETTER

Dear Ms. Name

I have been a (company name) customer since (add in the year), and during that time, I have enjoyed my experience greatly. I am writing now to see if you would be willing to make a "goodwill" adjustment to your reporting to the main credit agencies. I have two late payments on the account that I referenced above that date back to (add in the date here). Since that time, I have been an exceptional customer, paying all my other monthly payments on time.

Because of my exceptional payment history over the last X years, I would like you to consider removing the late payments from my credit report. At the time of the late payments, I was in the process of changing jobs. It does not justify why the payments were late, but rather there to show that these late payments are not a good indicator of my actual creditworthiness. I hope that (company name) is willing to work with me on erasing this mark from the reports.

I have been a happy and satisfied customer in the past and hope to continue a long relationship with (company name), as the credit industry is so competitive. I know how important it is to maintain good relationships with customers, and you have done an exceptional job in my book so far. I already highly recommend your company to all of my relatives and friends.

I hope that you will consider my request and prove, once again, why (company name) is heads above the rest. I look forward to your reply.

Sincerely

(your signature)

CONCLUSION

Thank you for making it through to the end of *609 Letter Templates and Other Credit Repair Secrets*, we hope it was informative and able to provide you with all of the tools you need to achieve your goals whatever they may be.

The next step is to get started with writing your own letters. Section 609 is a loophole that anyone can use. And even if you don't feel like you have that much of a case to start with, if the credit reporting agency doesn't get back to you with a response within 30 days, you can still have something taken off your credit report. Think of how simple and easy this can be. Rather than waiting for years for something to get taken off your report, you could get it off in a month or so, and get that credit score nice and high!

This guidebook took some time to talk more about debt and our credit score and how they affect each other. We took a look at the importance of a FICO score and why having a higher score is going to be the best thing for you. Then we moved on to looking at the worst things to do for your own credit, some of the best things to do for your credit, and even some of the secrets that you need to know to finally get your credit score to 800 or above!

Once we get a better understanding of what our credit score is all about and how this process all works, it is time for us to move on to some of the basics that we need to know when it is time to work on Section 609. While this is a loophole that anyone is able to utilize, we have to remember that a lot of people do not know what this is all about. We took some time in this guidebook to look at what section 609 is all about and how we can utilize this for our own needs to ensure that we can actually use it for our advantage.

Section 609 is a great option to work with when it is time to handle getting our credit reports cleared up. And we are going to work with some of the best templates that we can work with to ensure that we are able to actually send in the information about the incorrect or invalid parts of our credit reports, and get it all to match up and clear out, raising our credit scores in the process. It does take a little time, but with a bit of perseverance and the right wording, you can get it done much faster than what you would be able to do if you just waited for it to all fall off naturally.

Clearing your credit report and getting your score to be as high as possible is going to be important when it comes to helping us see success with our futures. Whether we want to get a home or have money lent to us in another form, having a higher credit score makes this easier to do overall. When you are ready to learn more about Section 609 and what it can do for your overall credit score, and you want to make sure that you are using the right templates to get it done and to get the credit agencies to work with you and take you seriously, then make sure to check out this guidebook to get started!

Finally, if you found this book useful in any way, a review on Amazon is always appreciated!

DESCRIPTION

A provenGuideonhowfixyourCredit in a Legal and FastwayandbringyouFinancialFreedom!

Are you tired of being rejected by the banks and other financial institutions because you have bad credit? Are you ready to get through and work on improving your credit score in order to get the funding that you need? What if you could write a few letters and attach a few supporting documents and get a lot of your credit score cleared up and ready to go?

That is exactly what this guidebook is going to help us do. We are going to learn some of the basics that we need in order to understand what our credit score is and how we can help it or harm it if we are not careful. But the crowning jewel we are going to spend time on is the idea of Section 609, and how some of the loopholes we can work with can help clear out our credit report and raise that score almost instantly. Everyone wants to make sure that their credit score is as high as possible, and this guidebook is going to help us get started.

There are a lot of topics that we have discussed on credit, our credit scores, and Section 609. Some of the topics that we explored in this guidebook include:

- What a FICO score is all about and why it is so important.

- A look at some of the secrets that you can do to increase your credit score.

- How to harm your credit score and why certain actions need to be avoided at all costs.

- The most common credit myths out there and why they are just harming you.

- How to increase your score to 800+ without having to wait years to get it done.

- A look at what Section 609 is all about, and how this is going to help you to improve your score in no time.

- Some of your rights under Section 609 and how you can use these to your advantage.

- Some of the things that you should include in your Section 609 letter to make it stand out and ensure that you are fully understood.

- Some of the best templates that you can use to work with Section 609, the follow-up letters, the Cease and Desist letters, and even some Goodwill letters.

There are a lot of things that are going to come up when it is time to work on improving your credit score. You can work with a lot of different things when it comes to improving that credit score, but nothing is going to work as effectively as the Section 609 loophole, helping you to clear out your credit score and get things in line. When it is time to work with Section 609 for your credit repair needs, make sure to check out this guidebook to help you get started. You will definitely be bragging to your friends afterward. Get this book and get started today; you will not regret it!